EXOTICA

Coach House Press

EXOTICA

Atom Egoyan

Screenplay © Atom Egoyan, 1995
Essay and Interview © Geoff Pevere, 1995
Photographs © Johnnie Eisen, 1995

Coach House Press
50 Prince Arthur Avenue, Suite 107
Toronto, Canada
M5R 1B5

FIRST EDITION
1 3 5 7 9 8 6 4 2
Printed in Canada

Text design: Greg Van Alstyne
All photos: Johnnie Eisen

Published with the assistance of the
Canada Council, the Ontario Arts Council,
the Department of Canadian Heritage and the
Ontario Publishing Centre.

The essay 'No Place Like Home' was developed
during a residency at the Arts Journalism Program
at the Banff Centre. Geoff Pevere thanks all
participants and faculty.

Canadian Cataloguing in Publication Data
Egoyan, Atom
    Exotica

ISBN 0-88910-475-1
1. Exotica (Motion picture). 2. Egoyan, Atom.
I. Pevere, Geoff. II. Title.
PN 1997.E96 1995   C812'.54   C95-930768-0

To Arshile, who was born with this film

Contents

9 **No Place Like Home: The films of Atom Egoyan**
Essay by Geoff Pevere

43 **Difficult to Say**
Atom Egoyan interviewed by Geoff Pevere

69 **Exotica**
Screenplay by Atom Egoyan

149 **Filmography**

No Place Like Home: The films of Atom Egoyan

by Geoff Pevere

> *'I figured out a long time ago that being alone was easier if you became two people. One part of you would always be the same, like an audience. And the other part would take on different roles, kind of like an actor.'*
> — Next of Kin (1984)

> *'There's nothing simple about representing a human being.'*
> — Atom Egoyan

In May 1994, they chanted Atom Egoyan's name from the steps of the Palais. The Cannes film festival's epicentre, the Palais had just provided the plush setting for the first international screening of Egoyan's latest feature, his sixth in a decade, the lush, nocturnal melodrama *Exotica*. The unsettling story of a bereaved suburban father's pathological attraction to a lavish strip club where a young woman disrobes for him while dressed as a schoolgirl, the film had clearly struck a major chord with many of the press and black-tie types attending the invitation-only screening.

Not that they were unfamiliar with or unprepared for what they saw. *Exotica*'s unveiling marked the third time that the 34-year-old Torontonian had been invited to unspool his wares at the world's most closely watched movie market. However, the earlier films—*Speaking Parts* (1989), about a hotel employee who obsessively watches videotapes of movies in which a co-worker appears as an extra, and *The Adjuster* (1991), about an insurance adjuster with a God complex—had enjoyed their comings-out beneath the dimmer spotlight of the Directors' Fortnight program. *Exotica*, a film as unmistakably Egoyan's as *Nashville* is Robert Altman's or *Dead Ringers* is David Cronenberg's, had been instead welcomed into the category of Official Competition—the loftiest of this hierarchically infatuated festival's programs—the first Canadian movie to crack the category since the deservedly forgotten *Joshua Then and Now* in 1985. (It is a measure of the irrationality of Cannes that its most coveted program has historically featured some of its worst movies. In this, as in other things, *Exotica* proved exceptional.)

As they chanted the young director's name, the largely European crowds favoured the pronunciation that, in film circles, is one of those things that still delineates the Old World from the New. Where, in North America, his name is invoked as A-tum e-GOY-an, on the steps of the Palais he was being incantatorially summoned in the manner common to those for whom Canadian movies are exotic: 'a-TOM egg-o-YAN! a-TOM egg-o-YAN!'

It was a distinction that probably mattered little to Egoyan who, as an Egyptian-born Armenian, is hardly European or North American anyway, and whose films are about the desperate search for something like home in an era when technology threatens to erase the idea altogether. After all, here he was, the most celebrated Canadian director of his generation, even if his films were much less well known and appreciated within his own country than they were among the spit-and-polish crowds this spring evening on the Mediterranean shore. A week later, the same Old World enthusiasm would further manifest itself at Cannes in the form of the International Critics' Prize. All a little ironic for an intensely self-conscious artist who happened to work in one of the least supportive film-producing countries in the developed world. So who cared how they pronounced it? Unlike most Canadian filmmakers, who never get to Cannes, the ritual invoking of his name at least clinched something few of Egoyan's colleagues back home could count on: he'd probably get to make another movie.

By 1994, the year he completed *Exotica*, Egoyan had become the most distinctive, widely known and prolific filmmaker in Canada's recent history. According to most filmographies, since 1979—when he was a 19-year-old student of International Relations at the University of Toronto—Egoyan had produced three quasi-experimental shorts (*Howard in Particular, Peep Show* and *Men: A Passion Playground*); five half-hour dramas (*After Grad With Dad, Open House, The Final Twist, Looking for Nothing*, plus a segment of the feature omnibus *Montréal vu par*); one hour-long drama (*In This Corner*); one made-for-TV movie (*Gross Misconduct*); and six theatrical features (*Next of Kin, Family Viewing, Speaking Parts, The Adjuster, Calendar* and *Exotica*). Not included on most official filmographies are several other episodes of American TV programs like 'Alfred Hitchcock Presents,' 'The Twilight Zone' and 'Friday's Curse.' Plus he'd been to Cannes three times. Not home turf exactly but, in the context of Egoyan's cinema of mediated homelessness, close enough.

The same weekend *Exotica* was screened at Cannes, I was at a hotel in Orlando, Florida, attending a junket for a movie that would never be confused with any of Egoyan's. There I met an Austrian journalist on assignment for a New York magazine. Learning I was from Toronto, she asked if I'd ever seen 'a-TOM egg-o-YAN.' You bet, I said—even *knew* the guy. She was speechless and, for a heady moment, I too was catapulted to the ranks of the exalted. Along with David Cronenberg, Egoyan has assumed the stature of English Canada's most famous director. His stylized studies of electronic-age ennui have earned him regular berths at such other coveted off-shore movie supermarkets as Berlin, New York and Moscow. He's even been to Palm Springs, where he and co-invitee Denys Arcand were photographed flanking Mayor Sonny Bono. European critics have been collaborating on books about him. One sample excerpt, titled 'The Recollection of Scattered Parts' by Jacinto Legeira, from the 1993 volume *Atom Egoyan*, reads: 'But although mechanical recording is related to a memory circuit objectified by the distancing inherent to the machine in use (camera, video device), still the agent or victim of the stored-up images struggles to keep memory alive through his or her choices, despite the power of memorization.'

Such high-calorie intellectual enthusiasm is common. Like countrymen Marshall McLuhan, Glenn Gould and Michael Snow—each pretty self-conscious himself—Egoyan is a driven form-buster with international egghead credibility to burn. And like those fellow travellers on the Canadian intellectual fringe, his notoriety abroad pretty well forced his celebrity at home. In 1987, the year Egoyan made *Family Viewing*, a formally rigorous comedy about a young man's electronic-era revolt against the values of his WASP-patriarch father, the unmistakably non-WASP Egoyan received the most promotable boost to his career thus far. The same autumn that Toronto critics Jay Scott and John Harkness dismissed the 27-year-old's movie ('literal, intolerant and sentimental,' wrote *The Globe and Mail*'s Scott; 'no action and no sex,' wrote *Now*'s Harkness), German director Wim Wenders handed the $5,000 prize he'd been awarded for *Wings of Desire* at Montreal's Festival of New

EXOTICA

Cinema and Video to an effusively grateful and genuinely surprised Egoyan. 'This is a great honour,' said Wenders that November day. 'But I ask you to put the name of my Canadian colleague Atom Egoyan on the prize.' It became a core event in the filmmaker's mythology and—in terms so typically Canadian they command the status of national cliché—another demonstration of the importance of Canadians securing some off-shore support to maintain artistic survival at home.

Take the case of *Calendar*. Made in 1992, one of his best-liked movies wouldn't even exist if not for the intervention of European (and again German) generosity. Shot in Armenia, *Calendar* was born of a windfall. After receiving a production grant from the Moscow Film Festival, which came with the condition that any film produced with it must be made on Soviet soil, Egoyan decided to make a movie in Soviet Armenia, which he'd never visited. Then came the collapse of the U.S.S.R., and with it the drastic devaluation of Soviet currency, and Egoyan's production grant was reduced to loose rubles. Originally planning to scuttle the project, the filmmaker decided to push on once the German broadcaster ZDF offered to bankroll the production. Ironically, while *Calendar* was never intended for theatrical release, early post-production screenings went so well the film opened commercially to the most successful Canadian run of any Egoyan movie before the commercial breakthrough of *Exotica* in 1995.

Yet, for all his European cachet, imposing gifts and still-expanding reputation as the Canadian moviemaker who matters most, Egoyan's rapid rise must be credited as much to timing as to talent. He works in Canada, after all, where there is no proportionate relationship between skill and reputation or ability and visibility. To closely study the history of Canadian movies is to scan a grim roll-call of superbly talented and promising strays: Don Shebib, Frank Vitale, John Paizs, William Fruet, Leon Marr, Paul Almond, Claude Jutra, Ralph Thomas, Francis Mankiewicz.... The largest looming professional question in our industry isn't 'What are they doing next?', it's 'Where the hell did they go?'

Egoyan, who has been steadily scaling the sheer face of Canadian cultural consciousness for a decade now, has essayed an ascent that depends as much upon the cunning exploitation of changing economic and political circumstances as it does on the fact of raw talent. Brilliant, distinct and resonant though his work often is, it might have never taken root at another juncture in Canada's high-casualty history of moviemaking. Egoyan's was a rise that could well be titled 'Rule-Proving Exception: How to Get Ahead in Canadian Movies in the '80s.' Not that the whimsical properties of luck or talent had nothing to do with that climb, just that neither alone can keep a Canadian filmmaker aloft for long. Egoyan's timing and judgement have proven as impeccably precise as his artistic practice, which is pretty well what it takes to keep from falling off.

If you pay attention to such things, you likely first heard that ear-catching name in 1984, the year *Next of Kin* debuted at the Toronto Festival of Festivals. Budgeted at only $37,000, *Next of Kin* was partially financed with money obtained from the sale of the short drama *Open House* to the Canadian Broadcasting Corporation (CBC). The first step was thus taken in a process of incremental expansion that, in both creative and economic terms, would cast the filmmaker as the standard-bearer for English-Canadian film production in the post-tax-shelter period. Like *Family Viewing*, which followed, *Next of Kin*'s scant production budget was largely financed with funds from Canadian provincial and federal arts councils, institutions whose emphasis on the support of artists over projects would, to a large extent, make the ensuing auteurist tendency of Anglo-Canadian cinema possible. ('We're all babies of the arts councils,' Egoyan has said of the burgeoning Anglo-Canadian auteurist movement he leads.) *Next of Kin*'s release also corresponded with the inauguration of the Ontario Film Development Corporation, which quickly began citing it as the model for the kind of movie the new funding agency was created to support. Subsequently, the OFDC would supply funds for all the rising star's features, and Egoyan would become the poster boy for the agency's artist-first funding principles. Later on, the same system of public grants and provincial funds would contribute as significantly to the first features of Guy Maddin (*Tales from the Gimli Hospital*), Bruce McDonald (*Roadkill*) and Patricia Rozema (*I've Heard the Mermaids Singing*).

It must be stressed, then, that to speak of the success of a filmmaker like Egoyan is certainly not to speak of flush bank accounts and flash cars. The Canadian system of funds and grants is absolutely necessary in a country where the commercial film market is so cruelly skewed against domestic product. Without such subsidies, we would very likely have no film culture whatsoever. It is also a system that tends to support artists over projects, which of course facilitates the development of a kind of movie whose appeal will, by definition, be limited. Art films rarely bust blocks.

The '84 Toronto film festival marked *Next of Kin*'s unveiling before a paying public. Though the festival had existed since 1976, Egoyan's film was being featured as part of a new and rather skeptically regarded program called Perspective Canada. Devised by the festival's then executive director S. Wayne Clarkson, programmer (and later executive director) Piers Handling and critic and professor Peter Harcourt, the Perspective Canada concept would have been obvious in almost any country but its own, where it was considered risky. Selected from the current crop of home-made shorts, features and documentaries, the program was designed as a showcase for the best in new Canadian cinema. *Next of Kin*'s screening marked the beginning of a long public association between Egoyan and the Perspective Canada program, though it is difficult to determine who benefited more, Egoyan for the early spotlight the program offered, or the festival for the opportunity to claim the up-and-coming auteur as its own discovery.

Over the years, a lot of people would feel proprietary about Atom Egoyan. He's one of the most liked and respected figures in the Toronto film industry, which is no mean feat when one considers the deliberately indecipherable and downbeat nature of his films and the laceratingly competitive nature of Canada's busiest film centre. Even when John Harkness, writing for the Toronto weekly *Now* and easily the country's roughest critic on Canadian films, shrugged off Egoyan's *Family Viewing* on the grounds that 'I honestly do not think he has talent as a filmmaker,' he was careful to warm up to the slam by assuring readers that 'I like Egoyan as a person.' With arid courtesy, the filmmaker responded in *Now*'s pages. 'A note of thanks to John Harkness ... I find it refreshing that a professional journalist can use his lofty position to make such a moving gesture of friendship. I like you too John. No review attached.'

Four years after Wenders' famous gesture of admiration, Egoyan practiced the same symmetry in life that he imposes on his films. In 1991, he gave away his own $25,000 prize, awarded by the Festival of Festivals for *The Adjuster*, to a virtually unknown young Canadian filmmaker named John Pozer, whose debut feature *The Grocer's Wife*—an arrestingly original, no-budget study in male sexual dread—moved Egoyan as he'd once moved Wenders.

Also bear in mind that Canadians are alleged to harbour deep resentment towards anyone who's garnered as much international acclaim as Egoyan. Yet he seems borne above such earthly resentment by his modesty and curiosity. In a room full of people fresh from one of his films, the curly-haired, bespectacled director seeks everyone's opinion, and seems to take all of them to heart. Reactions to his films never fail to mystify or obsess him. 'I like the pain of watching the film with an audience,' he once said of his habit of sitting through screenings of his own pictures. When *Next of Kin* enjoyed a brief week's run at the Carlton cinemas in Toronto in 1984, Egoyan—who'd paid for his tickets—spent hours in the theatre's back row, wired to every response. 'One Tuesday afternoon,' he remembered in 1987, 'there was only one guy in the theatre besides myself. I was sitting in the back, watching him in terror. Every time he shifted in his seat, my heart would leap with joy.' Egoyan is generous when it comes to donating his celebrity to causes, usually cinematic in nature, that he supports. In 1994, in the midst of completing post-production work on *Exotica*, a movie that percolates with intimations of forbidden sexual desires, he wrote a letter to the Ontario Film and Video Review Board, the same scissor-happy organisation he had eviscerated in *The Adjuster*. His purpose was to protest the organisation's proposed banning of the controversial Japanese film *Tokyo Decadence*. Faced with this and other objections—Oliver Stone wrote too—the board modified its decision.

Though intensely busy and intimidatingly prolific, Egoyan can be spotted anywhere there's something he considers worth supporting. He and I once met at a CBC reception announcing a new late-night series of Canadian movies—he'd just made a brief but gracious speech thanking the CBC for its support (overdue though it was) of national cinema—and on another occasion he offered to speak to a tiny class in introductory film appreciation I was teaching evenings at a downtown Toronto community college. Later, after labouring for an hour to disentangle *Family Viewing* for the perplexed students, he thanked *me*.

Likewise, in September 1989, Egoyan rescued the Canadian debut of *Speaking Parts* from disaster. In a jammed and airlessly hot auditorium on the opening night of the Toronto festival's Perspective Canada program, the film unspooled with a reel missing. After excruciating delays just getting the movie on the screen—the management claimed the breakdown of the air-conditioning system was interfering with the projector—the audience emitted a low animal groan when the lights went up prematurely. Revolt seemed imminent. Egoyan stood up and thanked the perspiration-soaked crowd for its patience, promising the screening would resume momentarily. He then bolted from the theatre, hopped into a cab and raced home for his own print of the film. Upon returning, he was cheered by an audience who by rights should have been tearing up seats and hurling them at the screen.

For all his renown and respect, and his trivia-test status as the

EXOTICA

youngest 'Best Director' nominee at the Academy of Canadian Cinema and Television's 'Genie Awards,' he had been, until *Exotica*'s impressive sweep of eight Genies in 1995, largely ignored by the country's official awards event. Still, he maintained visible support of the principle behind the annual ceremony, which grants awards based on a peer-group voting system similar to the Academy Awards. In 1993, the year the popular, improvised and unscripted *Calendar* was released, it received a scant two nominations—one of which was for best script. Nevertheless, that same year, Egoyan sat uncomplaining on the jury for the first annual presentation of the Claude Jutra Award for achievement by a first-time feature director. Dark hair and modest height aside, you'd never mistake him for Quebec's famously hot-tempered *enfant terrible*—and the director of *Léolo*—Jean-Claude Lauzon.

Egoyan is a compulsive moviegoer, every bit as likely to be seen at standard-issue Hollywood schlock as he is at Bresson retrospectives. Leaving one of these big-budget time-wasters, which represent precisely the form of seductively vacant distraction his own films are so deeply suspicious of, he'll often say what he once said after a Hollywood drama about hopelessly attractive junkie narcs: 'I really enjoy movies like this, I just don't know how to make them.'

The movies he does know how to make are as unlike Hollywood as his family home of Victoria, British Columbia, is unlike Los Angeles. They set out to thwart the kind of easy emotional investment that Hollywood entertainment defines as essential, and their relation to audiences is, when not merely challenging, often downright confrontational. 'What I try to do,' he has claimed, 'is make an audience question their own reasons for watching it.' Not that he is simply driven, as so many avant-garde filmmakers allegedly are, to masochistically inflict pain on the same taxpayers who pretty well make his professional life possible. For him, the process of radically reconfiguring commercial film language, of making us question our reasons for watching his movies, simply re-poses the most essential questions of our cinema, questions as elementary to our movies as the assertion of triumphant individualism is to Hollywood: 'Who are we anyway? And where is here?'

In this, Egoyan fits smack into an impressively tenacious Canadian cultural tradition of epistemological doubt. The difference—and this is what qualifies him as the most important Canadian filmmaker of his generation—is that where most previous Canadian filmmakers had framed the questions in largely literal terms by making movies about people unsure of who or where they were, or in limited formal terms that countered commercial seamlessness with open-ended documentary convention, Egoyan frames the investigation in primarily formal terms. Moreover, opaque as his work often initially seems, his motivations for such an approach are less theoretical than practical. For Egoyan, there is no disentangling who we are from the issue of what makes what we know possible: you can't know who you are until you know what you know. Since, in the age of electronic representation, practically all that we know or can know of the world is what is represented in media, to ask what kind of knowledge media makes possible *is* to ask who we are.

Where we are is also radically reconfigured. In Egoyan's films, media become environment. Since he sees experience as something circumscribed entirely by mediated message systems, his films are about people whose very existence depends on the media that make experience possible. This possibly explains one of his most recurrent images: people watching. People watching screens, monitors, photographs, mirrors, and—the only thing that acts as a constant, if often baffling, assertion of individuality—their own flesh.

His films are thus about watching mediated events like movies, which is something he won't allow his audience to stop considering. In this, as in many other regards, his work is acutely self-conscious. You cannot watch his films without entering into a deliberately unsettling exchange about the morality and consequences of mass-mediated representation—without, that is, asking fundamental questions about why you watch in the first place. Which is, needless to say, exactly the opposite of what most commercial movies want you to do: their very existence depends on the determined effacement of such considerations. Their aim is the contented state of suspended disbelief. Egoyan's aim is for a state of sustained skepticism—suspended belief.

But Egoyan's self-consciousness isn't restricted to the screen. Not only do his films compel constant and critical consideration of our role as viewers, he himself engages in a perennial struggle with the moral consequences of his function as a filmmaker. Apart from Jean-Luc Godard, there may be no other director so systematically critical of his own practice as Egoyan. In interviews, he relentlessly wrestles with his own right to be doing what he's doing, and constantly demands our critical scrutiny of the work he produces. 'I'm at once very suspicious of why I make movies, but also very seduced by the idea of making images,' he told the American magazine *Film Threat* in 1993. 'And I think that tension is evident when you watch the movies. I find it's not an innocent process for me. There's nothing simple about representing people.' Nor about being so self-scrutinizing. 'When you start questioning your own function,' he told Jay Scott in an explanation of the main character of *The Adjuster*, 'it can be terrifying.'

Such concerns point to the fundamental experiential distinction between Egoyan and the Canadian filmmakers who came before him. As a film-literate, postmodern artist who neither went to film school ('the worst thing I could have done') nor trained at the National Film Board, Egoyan's interest in mediated identity has bumped the terms of the who-and-where-we-are investigation to a formal level few Canadian filmmakers have even attempted. (The noteworthy exception is *Videodrome*, a film made by David Cronenberg in 1982 just as Egoyan's career was plugging in, and which seems to have had a profound impact on him.)

Tracking the core questions of the country's cinema—who and where, individually and collectively, people living in this peculiar confederation are—Egoyan has cut an alternative route along the traditional paths of Canadian self-doubt. His contribution, as well as his challenge, is to have recognised that the questions aren't worth asking unless one frames them in the context of what makes knowledge possible in a post-literate visual culture. To watch his films is to enter a process of self-examination that can be every bit as perplexing and disorienting for us as it is for his characters. Then we're right where Egoyan needs us in order to even pose such questions, which is the same place he had that lone cinema patron at *Next of Kin*: watching his movie as he watches us.

If there is a dramatic device in Egoyan's films that helps shift the who-and-where-are-we questions from dramatic concerns to formal ones, it's imposture: people playing roles to conceal their own lack of certainty. In Egoyan's films, identity itself is malleable, to be borrowed, customized or invented by anyone with the motivation or means to do so. And this is a world where both motivation and means are abundant, where everyone seems engaged in a desperate attempt to connect with some form of meaningful, direct experience and where technology has made possible the constant splintering and reassembling of self, creating a rat's-maze cycle of the making and unmaking of identity.

Technology is one of the central issues of Egoyan's cinema, and one whose consequences are investigated in moral and formal terms, which for him are inextricable. Technology 'has the tremendous capacity to either trivialize experience or enhance it, depending on how we decide to use it,' he has said. 'I'm not condemning it. I'm just concerned about its misuse, particularly when instruments enshrine sentiment—a camera, a projector, a slide projector, a videotape monitor. These are bits of technology which the industry has told us can make the memories "come alive." What a potent dramatic device!'

Technology makes disguises possible, but it also enhances the fragility of pretence, for identity becomes as erasable as videotape or as ephemeral as battery power. This is a contradiction that paralyzes nearly all of Egoyan's characters, a contradiction that can be comic or tragic but can never be avoided. In his films, to pretend may be futile, but at least it constitutes a form of action, and often the only form available in such a spiritually and culturally inert universe. 'For 23 years I've been raised as my parents' pride and joy,' says the hero of *Next of Kin*, who's just decided to pretend he's someone else's pride and joy. 'That's got to change. I want control now.' Significantly, role-playing, as well as the eminently adjustable nature of identity, are matters the filmmaker seems to have a more than technical familiarity with.

A pre-biographical word of caution. In interviews, the compulsively talkative Egoyan, displaying a perfectly reasonable distrust of the process of representation, has expressed misgivings not only about interviews—of which he's granted countless dozens anyway—but also about the journalistic practice of superimposing personal history over an artist's public work. Still, with all due respect for such concerns, they certainly haven't stopped him from offering some fascinating insights into the personal motivations behind the films. It is in the interest of providing context to an often difficult body of work that I've chosen to compile the following details of Egoyan's life, all of which were taken from the filmmaker's own archive of collected press material.

Atom Egoyan was born in Cairo in 1960 to Armenian parents, the children of refugees, who gave him the name of one of the universe's smallest known particles of energy as a peculiar tribute to Egypt's development of nuclear power. (When grown up, he would name his film company Ego Film Arts, a name derived from Ego Arts, the furniture store once owned by his parents.) When Egoyan was three, his parents, troubled by the intensifying nationalism in post-Suez Egypt, settled in Victoria, that WASPiest of Canadian cities. 'It was a difficult time for my family,' Egoyan told an American interviewer when *Speaking Parts* opened in the U.S. in 1988, 'and the notion of escaping into a dream family was attractive to me. We were the only Armenian family in the particular city I'm from, and we were isolated from any sense of community.'

Eventually, Egoyan's grandmother was sent by his parents to a nursing home in Montreal, where she still lived when he received his career-boosting tribute from Wim Wenders. Interestingly, the film that so impressed Wenders, *Family Viewing*, dealt with a teenager's attempts to rescue his grandmother from the nursing home to which she'd been heartlessly confined by his father. Speaking to an interviewer in the lobby of the Cinémathèque Québécoise, three blocks from the nursing home where his own grandmother lived, Egoyan called the geographical coincidence 'a very strange experience.'

The filmmaker has spoken of his parents' move to Canada as a rejection of their ethnic heritage, a pattern he would soon replicate. By kindergarten, the boy refused to speak his native tongue, covering his ears every time he heard Armenian. His parents gave up, and eventually Egoyan had so successfully banished the language from his consciousness that he had to learn it again as an adult. His talents nevertheless manifested themselves early and often, and by high school he was writing plays and making films. One of these movies was called *Lusts of a Eunuch*. According to Egoyan, it 'didn't endear me to the principal.'

At 18, he enrolled as a student in International Relations at the University of Toronto. There he developed a new relationship with his ethnicity, a relationship consisting of equal parts pragmatism and playacting, like many of the benign impostors he would create for the screen. In contrast to the conformist pressures of Victoria, the liberal cosmopolitan atmosphere of one of Canada's largest universities allowed him to put his ethnicity to work. He joined the campus Armenian society and played the guitar at one of the society's concerts. (He is a classically trained musician who adores Bach.) From an Anglican priest of Armenian background, he took lessons in his native language, which he then spoke to his delighted parents when he went home on vacation: 'The power of saying a few words in your mother tongue—to your *mother!* It was so emotional.'

He immersed himself in artistic activity while enrolled at the ultra-WASPish Trinity College at U. of T., writing plays, movie reviews and making short films. By the time he began *Next of Kin* at age 23, his résumé included 10 plays and five shorts. His ethnicity continued to play a significant role in the drama he later admitted he was creating for himself. 'I learned for the first time how you can use your nationality as an excuse,' he told *Saturday Night* magazine in 1985. 'You can play a role. I played up my Armenianism. I used it to create an identity. I used it cover up my insecurity.' He could have been reciting lines from *Next of Kin*, the movie that snagged *Saturday Night*'s attention in the first place. 'The way I see it,' says the bland pretender in that film—a WASP kid seeking refuge in an adopted Armenian family—'there's nothing wrong with pretending. It takes more effort to speak what's on your mind than to say, "Yes, dad." '

At school in Toronto, far from his family, Egoyan both chose roles and had them chosen for him. In 1987, he told *The Globe and Mail* that some of his fellow Trinity students treated him disparagingly as a Jew. Arriving at a Christmas ball, he was asked, 'Egoyan, what are you doing here? This is a Christian event.' He responded by returning with his academic gown worn as a turban. When the first play he submitted to the campus dramatic society was turned down, he wept. Within a few years, when his celebrity as a filmmaker would make him one of Toronto's busiest invitees, there'd be no more weeping over rejection.

Among those who have worked with him, he is as famous for his focused concentration as he is for his productiveness, and today it is startling to see how fully articulated his prevailing artistic concerns were even in the earliest films. It is rare to find, as one does in Egoyan's work, direct lines that can be drawn between the early shorts and the later features, but with him (as with Cronenberg), those lines can be traced with a ruler. *Howard in Particular*, made at U. of T.'s Hart House cultural/recreation centre in 1979, is a rough-hewn anti-corporate satire in which an aging employee at a fruit-cocktail company is ushered into an ignominious early retirement by a tape recorder. Like virtually all of Egoyan's work to follow, it's about experience mediated by technology, the insidious evil of surveillance and the dehumanized status of the individual in a corporate or institutional setting. (Another measure of the 19-year-old director's focused career vision must certainly be this implicit understanding that he was destined for self-employment.) *Howard in Particular* introduces the first in Egoyan's long line of glibly confident, management-seminar despots, who are usually incarnated by the cavern-voiced, rather swine-featured David Hemblen. In *Howard*, that role, which exists only as an emphatically unreasonable voice on a tape recorder, is assumed by the young filmmaker himself.

Apart from hinting at an experimental route not taken by Egoyan (who may ultimately be too interested in the popular allure of narrative to retreat into explorations of pure form), 1981's *Peep Show* is his first film to ponder the seductive treachery of screens: a young man, his image enhanced by patches of superimposed colour, seeks out a photo booth in a high-tech porno emporium. Anticipating some form of erotic entertainment, he is confused then enraged by the machine's reproduction, first, of only his own image, and then, of himself with a woman disrobing behind him—a woman who seems to exist only on the camera's retina or as a projection of the young man's desire. A beguiling *trompe l'oeil* about desire, power and the psychosexual impact of technological representation—please imagine the foregoing phrase in French—*Peep Show* is an often startling miniature sketch for the screen-centered investigations of *Family Viewing* and *Speaking Parts*.

If the concern over electronic representation is first found in *Peep Show*, then *Open House*, Egoyan's next film, mines veins that are then more deeply probed in *Exotica* and *The Adjuster*. The story of a young couple being shown a dilapidated Toronto home by a real-estate agent who turns out to be an impostor, the film introduces the first of Egoyan's long line of desperate pretenders. *Open House*'s Frank (Ross Fraser) is a benign sociopath whose pretence is fed by a sense of higher moral purpose. His showing of the home, which turns out to belong to his own, once-happier family, is motivated by a desire to restore a state of lost domestic bliss that might be entirely imaginary. (The past, as acute a force though it is in Egoyan's films, is more often ideal than actual.) Frank's family colludes in this: his mother (Alberta Davidson) play-acts the genial home-owner whose mask slips only when, standing in the house's overgrown backyard garden, she learns of the couple's plans to renovate. Upstairs, Frank's invalid father sits hidden in a room, staring numbly at a screen flashing pictures of his distant past.

Deceptively intricate, *Open House* addresses certain themes and dramatic situations that have recurred in Egoyan's work ever since: the malleable nature of self and home, the crushing weight of an idealized past on an imperfect present, the impact on memory of technologically reproduced images. It's also the first of his films to boast those treacherously misaligned conversations in which language proves hopelessly ill-equipped to convey meaning. 'I generally keep my eye on things from a creative point of view,' Michael, the young home-buyer, reluctantly tells an over-curious Frank. 'I *oversee* things.' Moreover, it's the first film to open the moral labyrinths that follow. In a development that elevates the film from a vaguely creepy short story to a comment on a cultural condition, Egoyan reveals that Frank isn't the only one making things up as he goes along: Michael, the self-described 'senior creative director' at an advertising firm, turns out to be a copywriter with a month's experience. Apart from his part in the afternoon's charade, he oversees nothing.

Quite apart from being a variation on the who-are-we-anyway question, this idea of off-the-rack identity, to be adopted or abandoned after the browsers have tried it on, is articulated in *Open House* as the quest for something like home, a notion as subject to alteration as personal history. Thus the mother's momentary dismay that the young couple are looking for 'an older place' to renovate. 'So you can call it your own?' she brusquely asks while walking off. As much of Egoyan's subsequent work will often heartwrenchingly demonstrate, home is an idea that builds in potency as it recedes from reality: its power as an ideal increases in direct proportion to its unattainability as a fact. 'Have you ever noticed,' a character in *Exotica* asks in a moment that offers a key to the entirety of Egoyan's work, 'that the things you want are the things that slip away?' In these films, there is literally no place like home.

Egoyan's first feature is about borrowed identity. *Next of Kin* has assumed an odd position in his *oeuvre*, being regarded in terms that must occasionally plague him in the same way Woody Allen's early films dog him. There are many who still feel it's Egoyan's best, and who wish he'd dump the heavy stuff and get back to it. It's an understandable response. Long on surface charm and easy displays of emotional intimacy, *Next of Kin* at first seems Egoyan's most uncharacteristic film and, with *Calendar*, his most effortlessly likeable work. 'An intensely accessible art film,' reassures the box description on the Connoisseur Video Collection edition. Yet considered in the context of what preceded and followed it, only the tone is really exceptional. Practically everything else about *Next of Kin* is as typical of the filmmaker's concerns as anything he's made.

Next of Kin is the story of a blandly disaffected WASP named Peter (Patrick Tierney) who presents himself to a troubled Armenian family as the son they once gave up for adoption. Like all Egoyan's features, it's about the malleability of identity when representation passes for reality. His natural parents, who are frustrated by the unemployed 23-year-old's habit of pretending he's living more interesting lives than his own, take Peter to a counselling clinic specializing in video therapy, where he 'sees' his way out. 'What do you do all day?' the therapist asks the soft-spoken, nicely dressed young man. 'He pretends!' snaps his mother. Peter, meanwhile, is far more interested in the clinic's video technology than in therapeutic relief. The counsellor, following an introductory briefing, wants to know if anyone has any questions about the process. 'Does that system hook up with a synchronising generator?' Peter wonders.

Asked to study the tapes of his family's patently unpromising sessions, Peter—who successfully fools a temporary office assistant into believing he's a doctor—mistakenly views a tape of the Armenian family, who have come to the clinic to try to patch up the troubled relations between the father (Berge Fazlian) and daughter (Arsinée Khanjian, in her first Egoyan film). Realising that the root of the trouble is the absent son, Peter leaves his own family to offer himself to the Armenian couple as their boy: 'This is going to come as something of a surprise to you,' he tells them in a hotel lobby, 'but I'm your son.' After expressing momentary surprise at how blond Peter seems, they take him in, and Peter begins the task of suturing his adopted family together. (It is symptomatic of his particular pathology that he can only do so while pulling his real family further apart.) The process fills him with a sense of purpose once only dreamed of. 'I envy therapists,' he tells the tape-recorded journal he often lies to. 'I mean, what can be more exciting than getting to know another family, trying to solve their problems? What can be more satisfying than giving direction to other people's lives? It must give one a real sense of purpose.'

Stressing the facilitating role that images have played in Peter's charade, *Next of Kin* takes up the issues of media, morality and the flexibility of identity that the subsequent films pursue in increasingly complex terms. But what sets it apart is ultimately superficial. Doubtless as a result of budgetary reality, which necessitated the use of location shooting, inexperienced performers and a practically non-existent shooting ratio, the film has a sense of lightness, airiness and effortlessness that—with the exception of the equally rigorous but approachable *Calendar* —only rarely resurfaces in Egoyan's work as it accumulates scale, stature and cost.

Scratch that surface, however, and *Next of Kin* is redolent with Egoyanesque issues and obsessions. The morality of Peter's actions, which he lamely justifies because they're making someone's life happier, is constantly questioned by the film, and there's no escaping the fact that, at bottom, Peter is really only a couple of pretences away from the role-playing mass murderer of something like Joseph Ruben's *The Stepfather*— a horror movie about another grinning impostor who believes he's doing the right thing. The difference is, the stepfather eventually kills the families he initially charms. Peter just charms.

Then there are those unstressed but quietly unsettling sequences when Peter is caught looking directly into the camera, as he is during the pathetic birthday party thrown by his real parents (which contrasts completely with the messy whoop-up thrown by his adopted parents much later on), or the moment when Peter curls up foetally on a table so that his new mother (Sonya Sirvart Fazlian) can hold him like the baby she once gave up. As she snuggles his shoulders, he beams a contented grin right out at us. While such scenes make no sense in conventional dramatic terms (unlike the moments where Peter looks into the therapist's video lens), they make sense conceptually, as an expression of the idea that Peter, like most of Egoyan's characters, is living a life circumscribed by screens. Or that life itself can only be verified by its recording. In a way, Peter's entire life is played to a camera, given worth by its value as performance: 'I figured out long ago that being alone was easier if you became two people,' he tells us. 'One part of you would always be the same, like an audience. And the other part would take on different roles, kind of like an actor.' Asked by the therapist what he thought of the tapes of his family's first visit, Peter responds more like a pundit than a patient: 'I thought you did a very good job ... of pointing out what the problems were. You displayed a great sensitivity. Very polished.' Like many of his fellow pretenders making their way through this world of mirrors, lenses and screens, Peter occasionally presses up against the limits of his own existence and consciousness. And since the camera is what makes life possible, that's exactly where he sees us looking in.

Like most of his subsequent work, Egoyan's first two features revolve around the spectacle of reconfigured families. In both cases, dissatisfied characters create new family circumstances after rejecting those they find themselves in. Family, like such ideas as home or identity, is offered as something ideal, artificial and subject to alteration—something that needn't be inherited, for it can be made. It has little to do with biology, an idea that isn't surprising coming from an Egyptian-born Armenian-Canadian who once told an interviewer that, like *Next of Kin*'s Peter in reverse, 'I really consider myself a WASP.' Besides, it is a world of representations, where images are a vastly more potent determining force than biology. Perhaps this explains the kindergarten-age Egoyan's violent rejection of his ethnic culture, given its complete absence from the New World chosen by his parents. It certainly begins to account for the ambivalent but obsessively recurrent instances of cultural and familial reconfiguration in his work.

In 1988, he told an interviewer, 'I think the family as a biological structure is suspect because of the psychological demands that are placed on an individual, especially in North America, where you have such a proliferation of different images thrown at you. The notion that you surrender yourself to a group purely because they're linked to you biologically is naïve, especially if those people have not attempted to make an emotional connection with you. I've seen many families that have made little effort to define what their responsibility to each other is.'

Paraphrasing Peter's birthday speech at the end of *Next of Kin*—which is in fact the birthday of the son he is impersonating—Egoyan said this about family ties: 'I'm suspicious of [the family's] structure. Sometimes it should be determined by choice rather than biological bond.'

By the time *Family Viewing* was released, three years after *Next of Kin*, the idea of lives circumscribed by representations had reached a more elaborate and rigorously formal expression. Egoyan has remarked that he considers his camera a character, but it's really only one of many technological agents that take on defining dramatic roles in his movies. After *Next of Kin*, comprehension of his work increasingly depends upon one's apprehension of this fact. The abundant media forms in the films are in fact active agents in the fiction. If you don't get the idea that they're as crucial, if not more so, in determining what happens next as the often flummoxed characters are, then it's hard to imagine the movies seeming like anything more than arch, postmodern conceits. (Which, judging by the resounding indifference Egoyan's movies encountered at the Canadian box office prior to *Exotica*, is probably how many Canadians *did* regard Egoyan's films, when they regarded them at all.)

In *Family Viewing*, the story of an oedipal conflict played out in an electronic arena, this notion of representation as drama is the structuring principle of the film. Van (Aidan Tierney, younger brother of *Next of Kin*'s Patrick) is a young man living with his control-freak father (David Hemblen) and sex-toy stepmother (Gabrielle Rose). He discovers, among his father's vast collection of home-made porn tapes, images of himself as a boy. On the TV screen in his father's bedroom—dad likes to watch himself mounting his wife—Van finds images of himself, his real mother and his grandmother (whom his father has exiled to a nursing home) playing in the same kind of sun-dappled backyard garden that symbolized an unattainable past in *Open House*. Shocked by the primal epiphany of the images, which he seems to be seeing for the first time, and by the fact that his father is wiping out family history by taping over it, Van (who had hitherto seemed only like an even less motivated version of *Next of Kin*'s Peter) springs into action. Enlisting the reluctant help of a phone-sex worker (Khanjian) whose mother is kept in the same nursing home as his grandmother, Van embarks on a campaign to rewrite and reconstitute the family history the father is hell-bent on burying. When Khanjian's mother dies, Van moves the body to another bed, creating the impression that *his* grandmother has died instead. This allows him to have his grandmother secretly taken from the institution and returned to both his real mother—whom the tapes have revealed as an unhappy ex-sex-toy herself—and, by implication, the sun-dappled garden. In the end, the father expires, his final staggerings coldly observed by the surveillance camera he'd rented to spy on his son.

The treatment of the father in the film, a character Jay Scott described as 'an evil enigma that should be destroyed, not understood,' invites juxtaposition with some of Egoyan's public comments. 'My grandmother was a very important influence on me because she was my link to my background,' he said in 1988. 'But she was put in a nursing home when I was in my early teens and I never could quite accept that fact. Then, when I was older, it seemed natural that she would be there, and that disturbed me a lot: that in the process of becoming an adult, something had shifted.

'So I constructed a story about a character who refuses to accept his own complexities as a human being and constructs a reality that he can control. His disease is his inability to confront his own emotionality, so he has the desire to distance himself and to control his environment, which is obviously reflected in his sexuality. The only element that he has no control over is the 18-year-old son who questions his values.' The quote is particularly revealing of the filmmaker's idea of who *Family Viewing* is about, and who is thus the subject of its circuitously navigated moral lesson: the father.

Throughout the film, Egoyan switches between images recorded on video and film, usually favouring the former for scenes in the chilly domestic arena of Van's condominium. Additionally, these scenes are often shot and blocked in the stiff, unnatural manner familiar from TV sitcoms, of which *Family Viewing* could be regarded as a nightmare variation. (The contrapuntal use of canned laughter, heard on the soundtrack as part of the aural environment of a home where the television is always on, is an inspired stroke.) Repeatedly, the camera is positioned in a high-angle medium shot, a signature Egoyan vantage that variously suggests public-surveillance cameras and the kind of institutional TV sets one finds in airports, bus stations or hospitals. Sometimes the shot literally takes the view of the latter, as Van reaches towards us to change the channels on the set his grandmother watches so despondently. This image of an alienated outsider to Canadian culture glued to TV—Van's mother and grandmother are Armenian—recurs again in *The Adjuster*.

In a manner only hinted at by Peter's occasional lensward glances in *Next of Kin*, screens literally become dramatic forces in *Family Viewing*, circumscribing the world of dramatic possibility for the characters and becoming the virtual geography of their existence: the screen upon which Van discovers his vanishing history, the TV screens in his home and the nursing home, the video surveillance screens that record his insurrection, but also the screen we are watching. In changing the textural properties of the images we're looking at, and the formal blocking of those images depending on their status as video or film, Egoyan forces our constant consideration not just of the artificiality of what we're watching (which is easy in an era of such jaded media-hypersensitivity) but of the ideological effects of those images. They are seen to set the terms of how we experience our lives, our past, our memory, even our sexual gratification. They are—to thicken the stew even more—epistemological: they set the terms of what we can know.

That knowledge, as Van learns, can only be modified through a heroic effort to seize control of the media themselves—to grab dad's remote and change channels. (Consider in this regard the bizarre but true climax of *Gross Misconduct*, the TV movie Egoyan made for the CBC in 1992, in which the father of doomed hockey player Spinner Spencer, armed with a rifle, storms the local CBC station to demand that his son's regionally blacked-out hockey match be put on the air. Shot by police, the old man's effort at seizing media control costs him, as it cost *Family Viewing*'s dad, his life.) The screen we the audience look at must be regarded with the utmost skepticism, lest we accept any mediated image as given, let alone truthful. In Egoyan's films we look in and, with rodent desperation, his characters look out. In between is nothing less than the malleable face of knowledge in the electronic era: the screen. The border of existence.

The conceptual origins for *Family Viewing* turn on a pun, but a pun that explains Egoyan's analogous melding of personal history with technology: 'the idea of generations in the family and generations of images,' he told an interviewer. 'In video you talk about generation, second- and third-generation video—an obvious metaphor for the way the family works in the film.'

In *Next of Kin* and *Family Viewing*, characters act on media-generated revelations by inventing new narratives for themselves: Peter by acting the prodigal son and Van by redirecting (almost in the filmmaking sense) the trajectory of his own history. He seizes image-making authority from his father, in the process retrieving a past and a future—an *identity*—he'd otherwise have lost.

The connection between power and representation emerged as the central concern of Egoyan's next film (and the first to go to Cannes), the austere and initially inscrutable *Speaking Parts*. 'There is,' complained *Now*'s John Harkness, this time keeping his personal feelings about Egoyan to himself, 'a conception of human behaviour, virtually unrecognisable as part of our quotidian actuality, that makes it hard to know what *Speaking Parts* is about.'

Rooted in the filmmaker's stint as a laundry folder at Victoria's posh Empress Hotel, Egoyan's third feature traces a series of mutually dependent but hopelessly unequal relations, contained within a luxury beehive of a hotel, all determined by the top-down politics of image-making. Lowest among the drones is Lisa (Khanjian), a repressed and hopelessly maladroit hotel employee so obsessed with Lance (Michael McManus), an unsuccessfully aspiring actor and one of her co-workers, that she ritualistically rents videos the young man appears in as an extra.

Lance, the ambitious object of Lisa's displaced desire, enjoys more on-the-job status than she, but it's the fleeting and fragile status of a commodity momentarily in demand: outside the roles people project onto him, he doesn't exist. Clara (Gabrielle Rose), the grieving screenwriter, sees in Lance the spitting image of a brother who gave his life in surgery to save hers. For her, Lance represents an opportunity to remake the past in happier, if entirely synthetic, terms. (These two characters share the most cheekily Egoyanesque moment so far, when they masturbate while looking at live images of each other on video screens.)

Clara, who wants Lance cast in the movie she's written about her ordeal, is subject to the most absolute form of power in this image-driven state, a TV producer played by David Hemblen. Unburdened by sentiment or desire, but controlling the material and economic means necessary to produce the fictions that sustain life in this emotionally arid domain, he's Egoyan's most sinister autocrat since that other malevolent imagemaker—also played by the beady-eyed Hemblen—Van's father in *Family Viewing*. Only more so, since the producer's power is not unseated by any upstart romantic insurrection, and he knows too well who calls the shots in the kingdom of images. For most of the film, in fact, he exists only on video screens. Cast in the movie that Clara's written, Lance naïvely tries to wield his meagre influence by insisting that the producer stick to the original script. Like an electronic Oz toying with a trembling Scarecrow, the producer reminds Lance how much the actor owes to the power that makes pictures possible. No pictures, no stories. No stories, no acting. No acting, no life. To wit, no Lance. 'People have always watched what I want to watch. You have, ever since you were a kid,' Hemblen's televised image purrs. 'Did you watch television when you were a kid?' Poor Lance isn't sure of the producer's point. 'My point is, who the fuck do you think you are?'

Like *Next of Kin* and *Family Viewing*, *The Adjuster* sprang from a deeply resonating family experience. In Victoria, Egoyan's parents' furniture store was destroyed by fire. He recalls the arrival of the insurance adjuster, and the almost mystical function bestowed on this man by the cruel whim of sudden disaster. The fire 'started off one of the most heightened weeks of my life,' Egoyan explained in 1993. 'Sifting through the ashes with an adjuster, coming up with an arbitrary value of things that didn't exist any more. It was very inspiring for me to watch this very ordinary person elevated to almost the status of a mystical god through this process. He was the angel of reconstruction who was going to rematerialize our lives.'

As rematerialized in the film, Noah Render (Elias Koteas) is an insurance adjuster who bears a fascinating resemblance to Peter, the self-appointed family repairman in *Next of Kin*. Similarly deluded, Noah casts himself in the role of domestic saviour to people visited by disaster. *Speaking Parts* ended with the tentatively reassuring image of Lisa gently touching Lance's face; *The Adjuster* begins with a similar contemplation of the potentially redeeming properties of the flesh. What's gone is the reassurance. Noah stares at his outstretched hand, his skin glowing orange from the flashlight he presses against it. Noah is often caught contemplating his own skin, though not from the sense of narcissism one might expect of a self-appointed saint. One of the most chronically disengaged of Egoyan's protagonists (who is really talking to himself when he tells his clients, 'You may not feel it but you're in a state of shock'), Noah is simply trying to find ways of getting in touch: with his clients, whom he often sleeps with; with his wife (Khanjian), whom he never sleeps with; and, most desperately, with something that feels like the rapidly disintegrating idea of home.

Noah himself lives in an unfinished suburban development with lunar landscaping and shelves lined with fake books, and the movie—the first of Egoyan's shot in space-stretching widescreen—constantly stresses the heartbreaking fragility of the structures, both physical and spiritual, we like to call home. Noah's professional life is in fact dependent on the literal combustibility of the dream of domesticity, and nearly all the film's characters are defined by their attempts at home-building in a world that offers little refuge from the flames of remorse. For home, like identity, is again revealed as an artificial and treacherous concept. It can be borrowed, altered or cast aside as easily as the suits Noah wears to work. Eventually, the adjuster's own home goes up in flames, ignited by someone impersonating a movie director, leaving Noah to contemplate the only dwelling he's got left: his body. Earlier someone—a true believer in Noah the angel—had said, 'The day is too short for kind souls, isn't it, Mr. Render?' Sadly, the hand Noah extends towards the flames at the end of *The Adjuster* is attached to the one kind soul this misbegotten saint can't even pretend to help.

Gross Misconduct, broadcast during prime time on the national public network a year after the release of *The Adjuster*, is Egoyan's eccentric adaptation of Martin O'Malley's biography of doomed hockey player Brian 'Spinner' Spencer. On the surface one of the filmmaker's most uncharacteristic works, in Canada it's also his most widely seen: TV does that.

Misconduct—which was scripted by Paul Gross, future star of the television series 'Due South'—at first glance seems a radical departure for Egoyan. It's about sport, which had hitherto only appeared in *The Adjuster* as part of a bizarre sex rite involving a football team and a wealthy nymphomaniac. It takes place in a realm that's conventionally and resolutely masculine, while most of Egoyan's previous films had suggested that gender is as fragile a construction as home, identity or the family. It depicts a world defined by momentum and action, whereas most of the other work had played out under conditions of contemplation and stasis. Perhaps most interestingly, it is the first of his films about issues so utterly and unmistakably Canadian. To so much as discuss hockey north of the 49th is to engage in one of the few modes of discourse that describes a consensual national mythology. And to embark on an exploration of hockey's allure and meaning within that national culture, as Egoyan does in *Gross Misconduct*, is to start poking beneath one of the few primally Canadian experiences the country has. But that's precisely where *Gross Misconduct*, which sparked much heated debate among Canadians (and particularly among disgruntled hockey fans), starts to seem less exceptional than it at first appeared.

In following the story of a rural rough-houser (played by Daniel Kash) whose life began in backwater poverty and ended in a bullet-riddled Florida pickup truck, Egoyan fits Spinner's sad and

EXOTICA

unglamourous life firmly within those persistent concerns of how social ideas like family, identity and home are constructed. Spinner, raised by a cruel father and a passive mother in the harshly remote environment of Fort St. James, British Columbia, may be one of the few Egoyan characters to have his role in life chosen for him, but role-playing is again seen as the only avenue of survival in a world that offers few others. As Spinner's father, played by Peter MacNeill, puts it (and this man, a combination of brutality and affection, is one of the most richly complicated of Egoyan's malevolent dads): 'This is it. Life at the Fort. You can live here and be buried here. Or you can play hockey.' The film casts the Canadian national sport as one of the few national arenas where transcendence is possible, where the reinvention of self is both attainable and allowed. But hockey, as the Old Man's bleak ultimatum suggests, offers more than a role to play; it's a mythical home for those for whom real home-life is a grind of hardship and disappointment. Like the Spencers. That Spinner ultimately blows his only crack at transcendence is therefore the point. Again, such ideas are revealed as chimerical, and Spinner is viewed as no less a victim of self-deception than Noah Render. Both wind up losing homes and families as a result of their inability to grasp the consequences of lives lived as hollow performance, and yet neither is capable of even imagining alternatives. So devoted are both men to the roles they have adopted, they cease to exist when the costumes slip off.

While *Gross Misconduct* is the film that most vividly showcases Egoyan's limitations—the scenes of Spinner's explosive temper tantrums may be the least dramatically convincing moments in a body of work otherwise defined by constraint—it remains a bold attempt to project hitherto intimately scaled concerns onto the immensely wider canvas of a national mythology. In fact, its most affecting moments are those when Egoyan's particular concerns mesh with the mythic potency of countless hockey nights in Canada. Whenever Spinner vaults onto the ice, Egoyan cuts to old black-and-white footage of the real Spinner in action. The result is the simple but deeply provocative suggestion that hockey is the national cultural equivalent of all those videotapes, photographs and other forms of electronic recording that poignantly obsess so many in Egoyan's world. While subtly reinforcing the film's own mediated nature, these archival hockey inserts compel consideration of the extent to which shared cultural memory has become a matter of shared televisual experience. For Canada, hockey as TV ritual plays a role similar to the representational artifacts in *Next of Kin*, *Family Viewing*,

Speaking Parts or *The Adjuster*. Thus the stranger-than-fiction climax to Spinner's story, wherein Spinner's dad is killed by police after storming, shotgun in hand, the local CBC station that has blacked out his boy's game. (Peering down the barrel, he snarls, 'I've got a serious problem with CBC programming.') For the father, they might as well have blacked out his son: it's the same thing. In *Gross Misconduct*, hockey is a collective dream, the televised arena of the national imagination. It is our home, our memory and the repository of our most idealistic fantasies, and finally as ephemeral as ghostly figures skating across dusty glass screens. But, as Old Man Spencer understood more clearly than his son, it's all we've got.

While *Calendar*, released a year later, is Egoyan's only unscripted movie, it's nevertheless a film of intricately structured ideas and concerns. Even if the film were only partially improvised, one still couldn't help but be impressed by the extent to which it economically finds new ways of articulating the connections between such now familiar issues as media and morality, language and culture, and representation and power.

The film that most directly renders camera as character, *Calendar* is also the most poignantly vivid expression of Egoyan's interest in media as primary facilitators of perception and experience. It depicts, in the most emotionally affecting manner of any of Egoyan's films thus far, the toll taken by lives lived as technological representation.

Assigned to photograph a specific series of Armenian churches for a calendar, a photographer literally hides behind the viewfinder while his wife (Khanjian), confounded by her husband's prickly refusal to enter and experience the landscapes he's shooting—and he, like her, is of Armenian descent—draws closer to the guide and interpreter (Ashot Adamian) who's showing them around. As he did in *Family Viewing*, where textural shifts between video and film distinguished the domain of the father from the outside world, in *Calendar* Egoyan cuts from film to video as a means of suggesting the experiential chasms between characters. But he also uses the frame of the lens itself as an analogy for the photographer's pinched world view. The husband (a role played by Egoyan but originally intended for Don McKellar) flatly refuses to step around and enter the action he shoots, for that would mean relinquishing control of the image. And that, as Van's father learned at the end of *Family Viewing*, means giving up the only thing that certifies existence. 'What I really feel like doing is standing here and watching,' the photographer's voice-over says. 'Watching while the two of you leave me and disappear into the landscape that I'm about to photograph.'

The lens is his cell and his life-support system, without which he can't imagine living. In fact, it may be more important than life, if life is something experienced most fully when shared with others. By the end of the film, it's clear that the photographer's wife has remained in Armenia with the guide, her husband left paralyzed behind his camera, composing the shots that record the remorseless drama of their marriage in melt-down. Living out the fate to which the control-freak voyeur may be doomed, he returns to Toronto to obsessively replay the footage of his own failure. As if that weren't sufficiently self-punishing, his primary social engagement seems to be with the women he hires for monthly dinners that re-enact the circumstances of the separation. In the most elaborate displacement ritual of any Egoyan film, these women, who have been as carefully selected as the calendar's churches, leave the table, go to a phone in the background and proceed to purr sensually in languages the photographer can't understand. He, meanwhile, writes embittered letters to the woman who left him behind—behind the camera. None the wiser, by the end he is playing electronic-age Sisyphus, endlessly restaging his own abandonment, nothing to left to compose but the circumstances of his own misery.

Exotica, the movie that left them chanting Egoyan's name in Cannes, marked a decade since the quiet arrival of *Next of Kin*—a decade in which Egoyan had made the Canadian cinema impossible to imagine without him. It's appropriate, then, that *Exotica* seems such a deliberate summation of the formal and thematic interests that preceded it, as though Egoyan felt compelled to take inventory of what had been driving him ever since, at Trinity College, he first started making images about images. Certainly, if *Exotica* is not intended as a coda to a particular era of aesthetic investigation, it feels like one. Like many definitive works by innovative artists, it leaves one thrilled but concerned as to the next step the muse might take. It is, in other words, a film that is utterly Egoyan's, but that seems to betoken a journey's end. By the time the long walk through verdant fields that intermittently punctuates the film reaches its destination, you're left feeling that Egoyan has as well. Now's the time to unpack or move on. Thankfully, one doubts he'll unpack just yet.

Set mostly within the plush pleasure dome called Exotica, where men enter nightly in order to have costumed strippers perform made-to-order dances at their tables, Egoyan's seventh feature almost immediately establishes a referential dialogue with the films that came before. The music, once again composed by long-time collaborator Mychael Danna, is a thumping, dance-floor variation on the composer's sinuous middle-eastern themes for *Family Viewing*, *Speaking Parts*, *The Adjuster* and *Calendar*. Cinematographer Paul Sarossy's velvety visual textures evoke the darker corners of Egoyan's universe, those voids the characters seem constantly about to be devoured by: the dark screening rooms and hotel corridors of *Speaking Parts*, the immense ceiling of blackness above Fort St. James in *Gross Misconduct*, the dimly lit motel rooms and accident sites in *The Adjuster*. In this most densely populated of Egoyan's films, many of the faces we only fleetingly see in *Exotica* are nevertheless familiar: David Hemblen appears as a philosophical customs officer, and Maury Chaykin—*The Adjuster*'s phony film director and star of Egoyan's segment of *Montréal vu par*—is glimpsed transfixed by a dancer on his table. The club's emcee, an unsolicited guardian to the young dancer (Mia Kirshner) who is the object of the most troubled character's desires, is played by *The Adjuster*'s Elias Koteas. The gay pet-shop owner, whose smuggling of exotic animals eventually draws him to the heart of *Exotica*'s darkness, is played by Don McKellar—the predatory nerd of a censor in *The Adjuster*. The club's owner (who gets the movie's best line: 'We're here to entertain, not to heal') is played by Arsinée Khanjian, appearing in her sixth Egoyan feature, this time visibly pregnant with the son she and Atom will name Arshile.

Dramatically, *Exotica* also establishes a potent—and, in a movie about the grip of the past, apt—sense of sustained *déjà vu*. Its dramatic structure, which cuts a psychoanalyst's path to the site of original trauma, follows the same trajectory as *The Adjuster*, *Gross Misconduct* and *Calendar*. Francis (Bruce Greenwood), whose tragic loss of home and family makes him vulnerable to the let's-pretend allure of club Exotica, works as a tax auditor. Like *The Adjuster*'s Noah Render, he is a listmaker who ascribes concrete values to abstract concepts, and whose alienation is encoded in the fussy meaninglessness of his job. Like most Egoyan people, he is a character clutched by the past, whose every attempt to purge or remake it steels its grasp. Almost proceeding from the point where Noah was left staring at his hand, Francis is dealing with a profound but unidentified loss in the only way Egoyan's characters know how: by using the abundant synthetic means to rebuild it less painfully. Like *Next of Kin*'s Peter and *Family Viewing*'s Van, or like the screenwriter in *Speaking Parts* and the photographer in *Calendar*, Francis is frantically trying rewrite his own story by playing protective father to a stripper who masquerades as a schoolgirl during her act. Like so many of Egoyan's people, he's an impostor, attempting to play a version of himself that could only exist if tragedy hadn't struck, which means someone who can never exist. And while *Exotica* examines synthetic experience in the most sexual terms of any Egoyan film since 1982's *Peep Show* (which is as much a miniature of *Exotica* as *Open House* is of *The Adjuster*), its most haunted moments are conveyed by a recurring, simple shot that's imbued with the accumulated poignancy of a decade of cautious and concerned representation. It's a home-video image of happier times, of Francis's lost wife and daughter smiling for the camera, until the woman puts her hand in front of the lens, both obstructing our view and laying a firm grip on memory. In all Egoyan's work, this is one of the most breathtaking and heartbreaking moments.

Like Francis, Egoyan's characters are repeatedly defined by this determination to intervene, successfully and unsuccessfully, in the narratives of their lives. Consider the screenwriter in *Speaking Parts*, trying to forge a fiction from the surgical sacrifice of her dead brother; Noah Render in *The Adjuster,* adopting the role of loving, responsible angel; the rich couple in the same film, playing their elaborate erotic masquerades; hoser deluxe Spinner Spencer in *Gross Misconduct,* adopting an ill-fitting role as a hockey star; camera operator and subject in *Calendar,* playing out the dying embers of a marriage; the characters in *Exotica*, practising labyrinthine patterns of pretence and denial, using the conventions of pay-for-play erotic ritual to sweep up lives scattered into shards of pain and regret. 'I just need to find a structure' says *Exotica*'s stripshow emcee who, like most of the film's walking dead, hopes a new narrative might ease the pain of an old one that didn't work.

When Egoyan's characters are caught transfixed by images, as they almost pathologically often are, they're not frozen by the high beams of a paralyzing force. They're confronting the contours of their own existence, the walls of their own cells, and trying to imagine alternatives. And since, in Egoyan's world, mediated images represent the limits of experience, alternatives are only imaginable through the manipulation of the images that make experience possible. In some cases, like Peter's and Van's, it works. More often it doesn't, leaving the characters suspended tragically between a paradigm of reality they've fled and a new one they can't attain: such are the plights of Noah at the end of *The Adjuster,* Spinner Spencer in *Gross Misconduct* and the photographer in *Calendar.*

Sometimes the characters are offered something that feels vaguely like redemption, if such a notion means anything in a wired but spiritually gutted landscape. Yet there it is, in the simple touch of human flesh that attains such quietly devastating power in Egoyan's films: Lisa touching Lance at the end of *Speaking Parts* (the original script of which ended with the line: 'It's just the stupid television. I turned it off'); the embrace between the tortured father and the club emcee—whom the former had come to kill for wrecking his fantasy—at the end of *Exotica*; even the hand contemplated at the beginning and end of *The Adjuster*.

Such scenes, with their inescapable suggestion that the redemptive power of human intimacy is the only refuge from mediated experience, reveal the romantic imperative at work in Egoyan's films. 'If you have to sum it up,' he once said of his work, 'love can still conquer all.' Ultimately, the films describe a condition of spiritual vacuity that is corrosive and tragic, which can only be redeemed either by the short-term solution of seizing control of mediation (which only works as long as no one seizes it back) or the long-term solution of returning to the emotional basics of flesh on flesh—which isn't easy. The catch, as characters in *Peep Show, Family Viewing, The Adjuster, Calendar* and *Exotica* know too well, is that the media themselves do a fair job of redirecting even our most carnal impulses, enticing us to watch others engaged in those acts of intimacy that might otherwise offer our only avenue of self-knowledge and escape. It brings to mind an image from Cronenberg's *Videodrome*, possibly the most Egoyanesque image ever to appear in a film not made by Egoyan himself, in which a television screen, engorged with the image of a woman's lips, inflates, balloon-like, to consume the face of the man watching it. Later, in the same film, a TV explodes, blood and entrails flying: television as flesh itself, and flesh as a construct of TV. As a labyrinth, it's a damned hard one to find one's way out of, particularly when the raw material of its construction is illusion.

One can't help but wonder what it must be like to produce films from this slippery conceptual ledge, considering that the subject itself is the damage caused by our narcotic dependence on illusions like films. This accounts for the subtly disorienting quality of Egoyan's films, their tendency, despite moments of wrenching emotion, to keep us at bay by constantly throwing up roadblocks to the process of emotional identification. They want to keep us from wholesale immersion in the fiction, as they regard that desire for immersion as tragic.

Egoyan keeps us at arm's length by several means, not the least of which is a singular use of language. (The first thing that is striking about those few films Egoyan has directed from other people's scripts, such as *In This Corner, The Final Twist* and *Gross Misconduct*, is just how talky they are.) In his films, language proves frustratingly inadequate for the articulation of feeling and motivation, and the movies reverberate with the dull thud of words and phrases tumbling uncomprehended from people's mouths. Often, the effect is comic, turning the inadequacies of verbal communication into the stuff of misanthropic farce. In *The Adjuster*, a green recruit to the Censor Board (McKellar), in the midst of reciting the alphabetized regulations for moral guardianship, is asked by his boss (Hemblen) if he lives at home. The young man is reluctant to answer. The boss tries to help:

'It's nothing to be embarrassed about. I lived at home 'til I was 35. It's very common in some parts of the world. Italy, for example.'

'Are you Italian?'

'Do I look Italian?'

'No.'

'Let's continue. "D"?'

Other times, the failure of language can be as frustrating for the viewer of Egoyan's films as it is for his characters, particularly when we think we know what it is the characters are trying to say. Even more so if we recognise that verbal connection could well be the next best thing to actual physical contact: something that might avert a character's downward spiral into alienation and remorse. The problem is, in the visual culture that Egoyan's films cast as the barrier to direct experience, language is like other forms of pre-electronic exchange; its capacity for meaningful communication is purely residual. To the uncomprehending listener in the films, they're often only words—more undifferentiated static. In *Calendar*, the photographer looks through a viewfinder at one of the churches he's shooting. We never see his face during the Armenian sequences, only the landscape framed by his camera. At this moment he is looking at his wife and the guide, both speaking a language that he cannot. The guide doesn't understand why the photographer will shoot the churches but not go near them; the photographer's wife translates.

'Don't you feel the need to come closer? Actually touch and feel ...'

'Touch and feel the churches?'

'... realize how it's made, constructed?'

'Hasn't occurred to me.'

'Hasn't occurred to you?'

'He'd like me to caress them or something?'

'You know what he means.'

'No. I don't, really.'

Words, drained of their expressive function, are additional agents of alienation in the films—more walls, and therefore better ignored. 'There is nothing special about words,' says Lisa, the hotel employee in *Speaking Parts*. She has learned to concentrate on the pictures, which is precisely what Egoyan's films, with their dead-end view of verbal communication, also compel us to do. Trust too much to the words and we're as lost as the characters. Yet by turning to images as a refuge from alienation, we slide perilously close to the same ledge many have already slipped over. For here again, as with language, Egoyan's purpose is to de-centre us—to make the most familiar codes of cultural communication, like verbal discourse and movies, as strange to us as Armenian is to *Calendar*'s photographer. Or as English probably was to a young Armenian boy growing up in Victoria, British Columbia.

This unbalancing is achieved by a number of means, such as the shifts in visual texture between film and video in *Family Viewing* or the fragmenting of the film image by video screens in *Next of Kin*, *Family Viewing* and *Speaking Parts*. Often, this disengagement is realized by the refusal to follow one of the most elementary rules of classical movie storytelling, the anchoring of the narrative in the point of view of a single character. In Egoyan's films, point of view is just as slippery as meaning. For example, in *Exotica* the main dramatic line is intermittently broken by sequences of people walking and talking their way through a sunny field—the past as garden again. The characters who appear in these sequences, the young dancer and the club's emcee, are the only people who could possibly recall these moments, yet the sequences are placed in the film to suggest not their memory but the grieving father's, whose murdered daughter the two figures in the field will eventually discover. The flashbacks therefore make sense conceptually, as the walkers slowly make their way towards the discovery that will draw the source of the father's pain to the surface, but not dramatically.

A similarly subtle strategy of disorientation is at work in *Next of Kin*, which opens with shots of luggage on an airport conveyor belt. It will be nearly half an hour before those shots are given dramatic context, but it doesn't matter. As images that introduce us to a story about transient identity, they're perfectly appropriate. *Speaking Parts*, *The Adjuster* and *Exotica* share narrative structures that unfold in even more sinuous ways, introducing us gradually to characters and situations whose connections are only slowly unearthed. In the case of the latter two, key relations aren't revealed until the very end. If you aren't working to keep up, you're likely to get left behind. Similarly, *Calendar* demands concerted

EXOTICA

attention to divine the relationship between the Armenian sequences and those in the photographer's apartment. By now, this anti-conventional narrative structure is an Egoyan convention itself.

In *Exotica* as elsewhere, we're never certain from whose point of view we're watching things unfold, until we come to realize that the only coherent point of view is in fact the film's and not the characters'. Again, this reiterates the notion of media as agents actively structuring the fiction—as total environment—not only establishing the parameters of what the characters can see, feel and do but making those characters possible: no film, no characters, no story. In the increasingly material universe of Egoyan's work, it is the film that creates the story, not the other way around.

By refusing to employ two of the most secure toeholds to the suspension of disbelief in the commercial cinema—expository dialogue and a coherent psychological point of view—Egoyan makes the passive enjoyment of most movies a pressing and problematic issue. This no doubt explains why so many people find the filmmaker's work strange, unsatisfying or (easily the most common charge levelled against it) cold. By forcing us to question the illusion-building roles played by language and point of view in conventional movie narrative, Egoyan violates the basic conditions for that state of uncritically suspended disbelief called entertainment. Which means that if his films aren't 'entertaining' in the common sense, they're not supposed to be. In Egoyan's universe of free-floating despair, the allure of entertainment is a big—very big—part of the problem: it's what keeps us apart. So what, if it offers momentary solace? That's exactly why it must be regarded with the keenest skepticism. As Egoyan, playing someone who's just observed his marriage collapse from the 'safe' vantage point of a camera lens, says in a passage that could well describe the entire culture of amusement: 'All that's meant to protect us is bound to fall apart. Bound to become contrived, useless and absurd. All that's meant to protect is bound to isolate. And all that's meant to isolate is bound to hurt.'

In what may be one of the riskiest dynamics ever sought between a fiction filmmaker and an audience, Egoyan demands nothing less than our constant skepticism: of the films and their meaning; of the morality of the characters within them; of the process of consuming mass-mediated representations; of the motivations and assumptions of the filmmaker himself. In the context of the mass—and massively uncritical—consumption of mediated images that characterizes late 20th-century culture, the films function as a lonely appeal to caution and reason within the cacophonous static of popular entertainment. And they do so not by scolding people for their gullibility or ridiculing their tastes, but by appealing to the innate intelligence they so obviously assume we still have, even at this late date in the electronic era. Egoyan's films wouldn't be such puzzles if the filmmaker wasn't convinced that we have the capacity for figuring them out—a process calling upon the same faculties of intelligence, engagement and reason that can prevent us from succumbing to the numbing inertia that crushes so many of his characters.

As long as we're willing to meet the films' demands, and as long as this country remains one in which filmmakers like Egoyan can use the various means of cultural funding to subsidize such a meticulously damning investigation of the moral consequences of mass culture—an investigation a commercially hearty industry simply wouldn't tolerate—one feels something like hope, even in Canada. It is, of course, a fragile hope, as it demands far too much confidence in the bureaucrats who administer the system that makes movies like Egoyan's possible. The rug, as countless of Egoyan's predecessors and contemporaries can attest, could be yanked at any minute. Then again, such uncertainty keeps everyone—artists, audiences and bureaucrats—on their toes, lest they get too complacent about an industry that, after all, is really no healthier now than it ever was. And it may be that lack of certainty that has made a sensibility like Egoyan's thrive, since it serves as a constant reminder that nothing can be taken for granted, nothing is what it seems and anything can happen—all concepts that may be as elementary, or possibly even as natural, to the English-Canadian world view as blind, take-charge confidence is to the imagination of America. In Hollywood, the industry speaks proudly of itself as the dream factory. In Canada, we're not even sure where dreams are found, let alone how they're made.

In *Exotica*, the strip-show barker assures the nightly gathering of desperate and lonely men that bliss 'is only a dream away. Wherever that is.' It makes one imagine that perhaps Canada might be a reasonably comfortable place for someone like Atom Egoyan after all, considering that he's never really felt at home anyway. Wherever that is.

Difficult to Say

An interview with Atom Egoyan

by Geoff Pevere

(The following conversation with Atom Egoyan took place on January 16, 1995 in the director's office in Toronto.)

As far as you're concerned, does Exotica *grow naturally out of your previous work, or is it exceptional?*

I can identify many of the concerns and themes from my previous work. Its structure and approach to the relationship to the viewer are inherited from my other work, but the approach to character is something I can mark to the origin of *Calendar*, where the characters seem more aware of the state they're in. They're able to articulate their pain at some point, and for that reason seem to be more classically identifiable.

This wasn't something I planned, and I wasn't aware of it as I was writing the film. But in terms of the collective response it's one way I can gauge and understand why this film has been a breakthrough: people are able to trust that these characters are more responsible for their actions. More so than the other characters, who seemed to be acting because of a director's world view or plan. I think that in that sense, it's a break. But I wasn't aware of that as I was writing or making it. These are things you reflect on later.

Certain themes recur in your work: the search for something like family, the impossibility of intimacy, the moral consequences of mediated existence. Are these themes you're consciously thinking about as you're writing?

No, I'm not, but I can't deny that the act of writing is a self-conscious one for me. A lot of it has to do with attempting to understand why I have to dramatise human behaviour or human actions—that whole process of chronicling the strangeness or the tentative nature of a meeting between any two strangers, or the way people within a family talk to each other. The moment you're writing it, you're putting it under a microscope and deconstructing something that many people would just take for granted. That's part of my writing. It's not ever something that flows out without some degree of distance. There's something fragile and very determined about the way people speak, and I guess that tone is obvious in the finished scripts. People are very calculating and suspicious about why other people are asking them questions or how they must respond. A lot of that is an attempt to deal honestly with my suspicions of my own desire to chronicle these people.

But underneath all that is obviously the passion to write and communicate. So there's a paradox there, and that probably defines a lot of the contradictions in the work. It's not like these people are content to reduce themselves to the almost robotic behaviour they display. They're always looking for something else. They seem to be confused or in pain over what they've reduced themselves to becoming. And I feel a responsibility to seeing these people through this process. I'm not content to just leave them there, and that defines more than anything else the shape and the movement of the scripts. It's a movement towards an understanding of why they're behaving this way. Some moment of contact.

When you're writing, do the scripts tumble out in relatively complete form or do you wrestle them into shape?

It's funny, because last night I watched one of my favourite films again, Woody Allen's *Crimes and Misdemeanors*. There's a case where structure is an attempt to clarify a thematic concern. If you're dealing with ideas and concepts that are full of contrary elements, you have to find something in the structure which mirrors that and puts the viewer into a state where they have to ask the same fundamental questions that your central character is grappling with.

To me, that's such a primordial concern I don't even think about it consciously. The structure evolves that way. It's not as though I have a linear story and then try and reformat it. It's just an extension of my own attention span. In the first drafts, you're so impatient just to get the thing out that you're constantly diverting attention from one scene to another. That makes itself obvious in the shape of the final script as well. But it's really not a science. It comes from an attempt to be honest about the material, and from an attempt to find a structure where you feel you're able to address the ideas in as organic a way as possible.

Do you like writing?

Writing and editing are the two stages I find most satisfying because you don't have the pressures of time and money that you do during a shoot. It horrifies me to think of what you're prepared to sacrifice during a shoot because you have to move on.

I love the fact that, as a writer or an editor, you have time to deal with problems, and I love the type of problems you run into as a writer because you can feel like throwing the whole thing away. There's the possibility to do that, though I rarely do. You couldn't even consider that on a shoot. You can't at any point entertain the idea that you're going to say, 'Let's just forget this shoot. Let's just all go home.' There's always the pretence of having to go through it anyhow. With writing I love the fact that you can just put your pen down, or turn the word processor off, and go for a walk to deal with what are really fascinating and compelling problems. Like how to determine human beings' actions. There's something almost perverse and sacrilegious about it all. I always find it odd to think that as a director, you're commanding the way human beings will behave. You're creating a universe where people behave the way you want them to behave. So when you come to a stumbling block, you're addressing something which is part of your own personality that you haven't really articulated. Let's say something all of a sudden seems too contrived. You have to deal with what brought you to the point where the characters have to do that.

So there's an *indulgence* to writing which I really love. I don't think shooting is very indulgent. It can't be: it has to be planned out and it has to be practical. Writing doesn't have to be practical, though there are writers who make it practical, who see it as something that has to be done between nine and one every morning. I've just never really worked that way. When I write, it's for an uninterrupted stretch of time. But that's obviously going to change with the change in our lifestyle. I haven't been able to write the way I did, but when I do it's non-stop.

You mean the change brought about by the birth of your son Arshile?

Yeah. I know what I have to do. I'm going to have to start writing in this office. This is the place where I traditionally tend to do business, but in the same way that I've scheduled time for this interview, I'm going to have to schedule time to write, which I've never really done before.

How flexible is the script for you once you're in production?

It depends on the type of production we're talking about. If it's a medium-budget feature film, there's not a lot of flexibility because you have to actually shoot this thing in 25 days. Which means you have to break it down, you have to have a tight schedule, and you have to say, 'This is what we have to cover between nine and one o'clock. We have to get this done by lunch and then we have to go on.' So, strangely enough, the ability to bend and go off in another direction is limited only to an ultra-low-budget film or a very high-budget film. In a high-budget film you can spend all day on one scene and really explore that. Also when you're working with actors whose schedules are really limited, you can't necessarily bring them into town for a few weeks of rehearsal. So it creates tremendous pressures to find as expedient a solution and interpretation to the scenes as possible. Unless you have the money, or the lack of money, to afford that indulgence.

I don't mean indulgence in a derogatory way. I just mean the ability to explore different things with the material and allow yourself to make mistakes and correct them and try another direction. The ability to let something simmer. That takes time and it's almost unfathomable to allow something to simmer when you're counting how much it's costing per minute. Though that does happen. It's a bit hysterical when suddenly someone freezes and can't do anything and the whole crew is waiting while you try and come to terms with how to get out of that problem.

While the ticking just grows louder.

Yeah. Some people find that type of energy very creative. I don't. My fantasy of my own talent has to do with this romanticized image I have of what writing's about. Before anything else I wanted to be a playwright. I just never found my voice as a playwright. In a way, it seems difficult to understand, but around the early '80s, as I was desperately waiting for someone to professionally produce one of my plays, I decided that I had to take some control over my own career. Why I didn't start a theatre company I can't really explain, except to say that it seemed less tangible than making my own films.

I'm now in this odd situation where I'm not quite sure what I am. I get these scripts from other people and I have this strange feeling that if I was to direct them, they'd become as anonymous as any other Hollywood film. I don't feel that I have enough of a vision as a director to impart something to those scripts that someone else couldn't do. I'm not like, say, Yves Simoneau (*Perfectly Normal*), who's this incredibly visual stylist. It's not my strength. On the other hand, I don't think anyone else could direct my scripts. I'm really something of a hybrid. I'm not a compulsive writer, like one of these people I've come to really admire. This country has a peculiar tradition of someone like Martin O'Malley (*Gross Misconduct*), who's a sports writer. That type of person who *needs* to write. Or Neil Young's father.

Scott Young?

Scott Young. These are the people who need to chronicle, who feel an impulsive need to give a detailed sense of what they observe. It's not even something they're indulgent about. It's a practical, matter-of-fact process with them. I'm *astonished* by reading these people's work because that, to me, is what a writer does. That's not what I do. I'm a strategist. It comes from a different source. What a director or a strategist likes to do is organise scenes and environments and people in a peculiar way or particular manner to communicate an idea. What a writer likes to do is immerse their self in the process of description, the process of chronicling. I'm in awe of that, but it's not what I do.

I think my reaction against it perhaps was because of my father, who's a compulsive writer. Not a particularly distinguished writer, but this is a man who has to document every day of his life. He writes pages in a journal and has from the age of 12. He has books and books detailing his life. I was fascinated but horrified by being raised in the presence of someone who had such a minute record of what every day transpired to become. For that reason I think I never really fell into that pattern. How about you? Do you write compulsively? You must.

I think I have to write. I'm never more comfortable with the shape of my ideas than when I've managed to successfully write them down.

It has to do with what we were saying about self-consciousness. When I was writing reviews at the University of Toronto, I recognized a formula I was falling into. It was easy to follow, but I became conscious of that formula and very bored with it. I'm never bored about the self-consciousness of the process that I described to you, where I'm aware of the fact that I'm making these people do things they would not otherwise need or have to do if I hadn't decided to put them together at that place at that point. As self-conscious as it is, there's something fascinating about it. It's the presumptuousness of it. How dare I presume that at this moment, this man's going to walk into this club, he's going to find this person who used to babysit his daughter and they're going to then start a ritual which, I don't know, could it even exist? Could it happen? It gives me some comfort later on to talk to a psychoanalyst who tells me, 'Yes this could happen.' But the fact I would actually go so far as to make this film on the audacious basis that I can make it work dramatically because I like the idea, and *then* hope to give it an emotional resonance! The fabrication of it is something which terrifies me because if it fails, it would just become ridiculous. But I'm addicted to taking that risk, and extending myself to that point.

It's one of the reasons I've become so disenchanted with the scripts that I'm getting now, which are very well written but where formulas dictate how far anything is going to go in any particular way. I really like that feeling when you're watching something and you don't know how far it's going to go. To me, that creates a tremendous amount of excitement. I've always been drawn towards something whose parameters are not defined by genre or preconception. But you can fall flat on your face by the same means.

Tell me when and how the ideas for Exotica *began to take shape.*

I haven't talked about this at all. I've always been talking about an audit, and how this audit was the starting point. Of course that's completely superficial and evasive, because no film that's dealing with the emotional issues that *Exotica* is dealing with starts with something as banal as that. It's really something I've been carrying with me since my adolescence, I suppose. Hmmmm. I don't know if I should talk about this, but I guess I should.

During my adolescence I was very involved with somebody whom I later found out was being abused while I was involved with her. That experience was very powerful and influential in the development of this particular film, because I came to understand how the sexual act is something quite separate from a means of sexual expression. There was a tremendous loneliness in the process of sexual communion. I never quite understood it at that time because I didn't know what was happening with this person. Yet I was trying to deal with a lot of things I was feeling when I was close to her. That confusion has left a very deep impression on me and this film, more than any other, was an attempt to work out the charade of sexuality and the possibility of creating a sexual environment in which the relationships were quite platonic. Plus dealing with things outside of that, like how somebody who is abused makes a parody of their own sexual identity as a means of trying to convince themselves that that part of themselves which has been destroyed is somehow not as vital as it is. Somehow they have to reduce it to something more grotesque than it can be, otherwise it becomes too painful to deal with.

That's the emotional terrain of this piece. I had never found a metaphor to express a lot of these ideas. The first scenes that I wrote were dialogues with a babysitter. I was really drawn to that, because it seemed to me that's the first encounter many adolescent women have with older men. It's something which by its nature is fraught with sexual tension. Just by virtue of that fact that a lot of the time you're being driven in a car by someone you don't know back to your home. To me, this was a powerful concept because there was a certain parameter and ritual involved. As the male driver, you can't be silent because that makes it too weird. You have to talk about something, so what do you talk about?

The first draft of this script was based on this very odd suburban community. It seems far from where it ended up, but in this community there was a weird sort of amateur porn group. They got together and made these *documents,* and the one thing they shared was a common babysitter. The babysitter was the link to what was happening in these people's lives. The audience never saw what was going on, we just had these various drives home with this babysitter.

Through these conversations one got a gradual sense of what was going on within this community.

A neat idea.

Well I wrote that idea and put it aside. Then I became fascinated by table dancing, because table dancing involves this strange opening act. Before anything begins, you have to get to know one another. But you're not really getting to know one another at all. A dancer's not going to tell you who they are and you're probably not going to tell them who you are, but you create a fantasy of yourself as they create a fantasy of themselves. Again, it's a situation where people are forced to communicate because if they don't, it becomes too weird. Table dancing is weird enough, but it becomes even odder if there isn't this preliminary introduction. I thought that was interesting because I'm dealing—in both the drives with the babysitter and the opening act of the table dance—with a situation where people have to speak to deal with tension that would become unbearable otherwise. That became the beginning of the *Exotica* draft.

Then I realized that in both situations I was depicting in the script, the rituals had already found themselves. I thought, 'Might it not be important to see how a ritual like this can begin?' That's how Thomas, the gay exotic-animal dealer played by Don McKellar, became developed. One night he shares a cab with someone who gives him some tickets to a ballet, and he goes to the ballet to scalp the tickets. So he finds a procedure and an activity which seem like a lot of fun, which is, why not pick up a date by having two tickets and finding someone to sit beside you? Then we begin to see how that type of behaviour begins.

Those are the things that went into the development of this screenplay. Then other things become apparent. Like the subtext. The big question with *Exotica* was, what can you afford not to make obvious? For me, one of the most powerful scenes in the script doesn't exist, which is the scene where Francis goes into the club for the first time and sees Christina, who used to be his deceased daughter's babysitter, and Francis has a choice to either run out of the club or introduce himself. How did that relationship get from there to where we see it? We don't know, but we have to be able to imagine it. Then there's the decision of whether to show that or not.

There's also the decision of whether or not to show what Eric and Christina were about. We see them at the beginning of the relationship, but we never really see them during the relationship. So there are huge decisions to be made as far as what to reveal and articulate, and what is best left unsaid. That's something you grapple with all the time.

One of the things that impresses me is when a dramatist is able to create a scene that's so noticeable by its absence, it becomes concrete. It's a bizarre example, but in Shakespeare's *Measure for Measure* there's an incredible scene where Isabella, who doesn't want to give up her honour, implores a friend of hers to comply with this sexual proposition that she can't respond to by having her friend go and meet this person in a darkened room and make love to him. That scene where they actually make love, where this man is so caught up with his desire and the folly of his anticipation that he fails to actually realize that it's not the same woman that he's making love with, doesn't exist in the play. Yet when I went to go and see it at Stratford a couple of years ago, I was waiting for that scene because I was sure it was in the script. But it wasn't. It's just such a clearly etched moment that I came to believe it was there.

To me, the highest aim of any film is to enter so completely into the subconscious of the viewer that there are moments and scenes and gestures which can be generated by the spectator's imagination. That becomes part of the film they're playing in their mind, and I hope the film has enough space to allow that type of room, that type of exchange.

I don't think you sit down and you consciously try and get to that point. If it happens it's wonderful, but there's no science to it. I'm sure there are some people who say that there must be some sort of alchemy involved in what you resist showing and what you give, but I haven't worked it out.

So how did you arrive at the decision not to include the scene where Francis first sees Christina at the club?

It becomes a question of rhythm. I believe, like Andrei Tarkovsky said, that film is 'sculpting in time.' When you're working with time, each period you're working with has its own rhythm. As you're mapping out a screenplay, sometimes something just won't allow itself to fit in, or it seems too predetermined.

One of the things that's great about looking at a film like *Crimes and Misdemeanors* is how comfortable Allen is throwing everything into the soup. There are scenes and flashbacks which are just kind of thrown in indiscriminately, but they work. Sometimes they're not very considered, yet the structure itself is so detailed. The way I work, it's difficult to throw away scenes. I'm too aware of what goes into the construction of a scene. So something like the field scenes [in *Exotica*]—which for me are much more dreamy or loose than anything I've ever written before—were something that I probably wouldn't have been able to put into a screenplay before *Calendar*. *Calendar* taught me it's okay to have scenes where people are speaking very naturally.

That's the other draft I wanted to mention! I was always fascinated by the idea of two people meeting during a search for somebody else, or the search for someone's body. I remember speaking about this to a friend of mine, saying, 'Wouldn't it be neat to have a whole film where you just saw a relationship develop during a search?' That was another idea that worked its way into this. But I'm not the dramatist to write a linear account of a couple's first day in a field. I would love to see a movie like that, but I'm not the person to write it.

I think my dialogue and scripts serve my particular designs pretty well. But there are people who are far more accomplished writers than I am and I'd like to be able to collaborate in such a way that I'm able to use my sense of dramatic and structural strategy with someone whose sense of dialogue is so compulsive—to use that word from before—that you can just listen to people talk and know exactly who they are and why they have a right to exist. Though that might defeat my structural strategy.

One of my favorite films is [Coppola's] *The Conversation*. Gene Hackman is the central character, a person so shy and withdrawn he seems incapable of talking, and he's eavesdropping into this one central conversation. You could listen to what those people are talking about in that park forever, yet what they're saying is so simply drawn out. But something about the writing of that scene is very compelling. And I'll never forget that moment in the film when Gene Hackman's at a trade show and he's suddenly excited about this new piece of technology. Remember that scene? All of a sudden you just know this guy *completely* by his enthusiasm.

EXOTICA

It's interesting. I don't think it's an unusual situation because I think there are a lot of other directors who write their own material who are—and it's an embarrassing term to use because it has so many other associations—'auteurs.' I'm referring to that idea of being able to use film language to create a form of writing which is distinct from, let's say, the well-made screenplay or film. There's a messiness to many auteurs' films because they're trying to grapple with something which is neither one thing nor the other. If I can speak for others, there's a sense of surprise that it comes together, followed by horror when you realize that you haven't forged any way of defining the science of it. It's a matter of dealing with a set of emotional issues that have provoked a number of scenes and moments and patterns of behaviour which you as a writer can't shake, which stick with you, that you have to put together.

It's interesting what you're saying about dialogue. Have you seen Quentin Tarantino's Pulp Fiction *in a crowded theatre?*

Yeah!

The way that dialogue works on people is astounding. It audibly thrills them.

It's fantastic. I think what people are responding to with *Pulp Fiction*, and it's what I'm in awe of, is that it gives voice to images that have crossed all of our collective consciousnesses, but we thought were too petty to actually chronicle: the way people make references to bad TV or things that don't seem to warrant dramatic attention. He's found this way of finding a poetry of language which is meant to deal with the minutiae of pop culture which has touched a nerve. It's really exciting. It's liberating.

Many people have suggested that Exotica *marks a significant departure from your previous work because it's concerned with a form of live performance as opposed to electronic reproduction. Do you see this as a significant difference?*

I was aware that the video image was becoming overworked in my films and was allowing people to reduce the ideas I was working with to a cliché, and that became something I wanted to avoid. Yet the idea of people making an artifact of their experience, an artifact which could be exchanged and manipulated, is something I continue to find fascinating. In a way, what I've done is gone back to a more classical interpretation of that with live performance. Instead of people having a videotape that one has to access and find the code to play, you have a uniform, a schoolgirl's uniform, which you can't just accept as a material artifact. You have to understand what brought the person to the point of transforming themselves into that persona. In the same way that in the other films, you have to understand what brought the person to the point where they feel the need to take over this image, or masturbate to it, or manipulate it in some way. What does it take for someone to have to do that?

I'm really attracted to patterns of behaviour which seem delusional and bordering on pathological but society has embraced as quite normal. I mean, it's normal now to create a chronicle of someone's life through video. What you've done by doing so is frozen and come to terms with very disturbing ideas of time like 'time changes' or 'time passes.' You're able to arrest time, to go back later on and demystify those concepts. The creation of any type of artifact, be it a tribal mask or the videotape of a first birthday, is an attempt to come to terms with something which is larger or more mysterious than our immediate understanding. That artifact in and of itself doesn't answer any questions. What was happening with the videotape in my films was somehow providing an answer to things I was raising. 'Oh, it's because the technologies are bad' or 'It's because these things have run out of control.' Or that we have to go back to a more primitive, basic sort of family unit. It's not as simple as that, yet people were drawing that conclusion, so I wanted to show that the issues existed outside of that type of technology.

Ever since the early short film Peep Show, *your work has demonstrated a concern with sexuality as an expression of economic or political power. This is also evident in* Exotica, *where it seems like all relationships are defined by the exchange of money. Is there such a thing as sexuality divorced from power?*

In any sharing of physical experience there is the pleasure of feeling that your pleasure is the result of a communion with another person or another body. The delineation between whether that's something engineered you're seeing through to its completion, or a spontaneous act of emotional response, is challenging to the dramatist because drama is something which by its nature cannot be spontaneous. It's absurd and a bit redundant to celebrate any act of sexual passion on screen as being laudable because it seems spontaneous. It never really is. I don't think I could ever entertain that illusion. The reason why any sexual act in my films is so predetermined and engineered is because I'm responding to what I feel when I'm writing those things. It's an attempt to understand why I need to create a sex scene, what it is I'm trying to satisfy in myself.

I used to think that if you created a really incredibly potent party scene that displayed to people you were a social beast, that you carried the seeds of that party within you. It's a folly that a lot of filmmakers carry with them, and I'm certainly a victim of it. For instance with

EXOTICA

Tarantino's work, if he's able to contain the seeds of such a reservoir of pop culture, somehow that makes him all of those things that people feel when they see his films. You can't even begin to believe that, because it creates this delusional experience where you have to see yourself as a glamorized individual. You have to remove yourself from that.

I also used to think that if I ever created a scene that displayed my sexual fantasy or fetish, I would have a document that would turn me on and yet would be somehow pure because it was the act of my own creative hand. Of course it's absurd to believe that, because as a filmmaker you're so painfully aware of what went into making that image, you can never lose yourself in it. Yet there's something fascinating about the fact that we do engineer sexual situations that we do lose ourselves in. Like what a fetishist or sadomasochist or transvestite does—these are people I'm in awe of because they're able to construct a fantasy and play it out *and* get turned on by it! Which I can't. My sexual tastes are so basic in some ways it's kind of embarrassing. Yet I'm fascinated by people who are able to extend their sexual identities into something it takes a lot of work to get to, and still at the end find the wherewithal to lose themselves in the thing they've made. It happens, but not very often with me.

The closest I can come in terms of my own sort of fantasy would be—let's say there's a piece of pornography that you're drawn to that you have on videotape. After a while it's lost some of its power because you've seen it so many times—it's so within your possession. Then I had this idea that to spruce it up a bit, what you'd want is to have it playing in a monitor in a room. Then you go outside the room and watch it again through a keyhole! So you've created this new barrier to get through in order to recover that thing which has become so banal.

Or hide it somewhere at your parents' place.

Or hide it somewhere. It's part of our whole generation, where our sexuality was defined by pornography. It's a very important thing to consider. Much like my son's generation is going to be defined by video pornography or god knows what by the time he's an adolescent. I have to confess to having a certain nostalgia for *Penthouse* circa 1973. It's sick and sort of disturbing, but something in me feels fondly towards those magazines, yet it's only because they were able to make tangible something which is completely ambiguous.

Much like there's something phenomenal about the fact that every night, every person in this world turns on a little projector in their brain when they go to sleep and creates *movies*. I'm still so awed by that, that we all have our own private *mise en scène* going on in our brains every night. In the same manner it's incredible to me that everybody on this planet has a sexual identity, and that what we consider to be so private and particular to our own definition or needs is something that everybody has their own particular way of expressing.

The intolerance that's around shocks me. I'm really stunned by sexual intolerance. For instance, because in a lot of the films there's a gay character, people have asked me, 'How can you have such a casual approach to gay sex?' I don't think twice about it. I don't think I'm doing something particularly liberal. It's just that I understand there's an incredibly wide spectrum of human sexual expression. Since I'm so unadventurous in terms of my own sexuality, I deeply respect people who are able to extend themselves and make their sexuality something more theatrical, something they have to design, follow up on and put a lot of work towards. That's really admirable.

It's like people who go to therapy. I've never been, yet I'm fascinated by that process and think if I wasn't making films, maybe I'd be a therapist, because it's incredible to me that people go and spend an hour every week or day trying to work out something. I have this sort of smug sense that I'm working things out with my movies, but I'm sure I'm just basically lazy.

That's what I really admire about my characters. That's why I like to depict these people. These are people who are doing things I would like to do sometimes. Sometimes for dark reasons I'd prefer to avoid, but they're all directors. They're all engineering other people to do something, and the passion and conviction with which they do that is something I find really striking.

The problem with creating your own therapeutic exercises is that there's not someone there to monitor it. There's no one there to tell you if it's going too far or if you're actually fucking yourself up. That's why I think in *Exotica* the character of Eric actually becomes a monitor for Francis, when he expels Francis from the club, which is apparently because of his own jealousy. But there's also something else. There's this sense that he's maybe giving something to Francis, saying to Francis, 'This is going too far. This has to be broken.'

Or the father in *Family Viewing*. The guy is such a wounded beast, but there's something human to me about the fact that he thinks he can deal with his past by erasing it over with homemade pornography. The level of imagination that would bring someone to a point where he has to call this woman to give him sexual directions so that he can then produce images that will tape over his past ... that takes my breath away. That type of thing impresses me, maybe for all the wrong reasons. I'm trying to figure that out, that's why I make films. I'm trying to understand what the nature of my attraction to those things is about. You have to have a level of fascination with the things that are going to be most morally challenging to a viewer. Otherwise you don't have that sense of what we talked about before, which is that this thing might go too far. You need that. You need that edge.

That's where filmmaking involves a degree of honesty which is frightening, if you stop and think about it too much. I've just been doing it for so long I guess it's the ritual that I've created around *my* life: every couple of years I assemble 45 people together and we create these scenes. That's my ritual. Straight ahead as my sexual life might be, it does have this odd kink to it, and obviously that has other ramifications when you're making images of someone you love, and distorted images at that. I'm sure there's a whole other agenda, and I'm sure someone would have a field day trying to break that all down.

And someday someone will. Do you believe that intimacy is as difficult or as impossible to obtain as it so often seems to be in your films?

No, absolutely not. I don't. I feel we are capable of intimacy, but our society provides us with so many things which seem to give us greater access to intimacy but in fact confuse the issue of what it is, and provide a substitute which then sets its own agenda. So when you have things floating around in your home or immediate sphere which have become artifacts of an intimate feeling or time, and you trade those artifacts as a kind of currency either with yourself or with others, the issue becomes more complicated.

It's not as simple a matter as it used to be a hundred years ago. We've just become more sophisticated in our definition of what intimacy is about. We have to work a bit harder at understanding what it is we're actually sharing at any given time. We've become a lot more self-conscious about what it means to be at the receiving or giving end of a piece of intimate information. At the turn of the century, a farmer would have an almanac and the information within that would be information he'd be able to use immediately. The information in and of itself didn't become something other than what this person needed to get on with life. Now we have so many bits of information which can consume our interest and take us someplace where we can be involved, but that doesn't refer back to our immediate personality. In the same way, there are so many things we can become intimate with, and so many feelings that we're invited to partake in or share, and so many forms by which we can express our intimacy. But what we ultimately have to refer back to becomes diluted in the process, because it's not as guarded as it used to be. It's not as defined. We're not quite sure what we're drawing from.

In Exotica, *there don't seem to be any relations between characters that aren't determined by some form of financial exchange or contract. That seems to be the obstacle which blocks any form of genuine or unguarded intimacy between them.*

I think the contracts and the financial exchanges are a way of making tangible that which is too terrifyingly abstract otherwise. They're able to crystallize and articulate the parameters of a relationship by a means which is easy to understand with the exchange of a bill. You've given me a service, and by the amount of money that I'm paying you, we've understood what that service is worth. And the moment we understand what it's worth, we're able to commodify it. Now why do we need to do that? Because otherwise it's frightening to understand what's brought me to the point where I have to even talk to a stranger or have a stranger dance for me at a table, or have to pick up someone at an opera, or have to drive home my niece who's pretending to babysit a child who's not home. All these ideas are otherwise so grotesque and pathological that by putting a price to them, you're saying they work within the everyday understanding of how we define a marketplace. It's a way of saying, 'Hey! This is quite normal, because I pay for it.' If you don't pay for it, it provokes a whole other set of questions which I don't think these people are prepared to deal with. Like how do you repay someone for generosity of spirit? How do you actually become generous of spirit with somebody whose motivations are morally suspect? These people don't have to ask those questions because at some level, those questions are being curtailed by the exchange of notes.

It's no exaggeration to say that in the past 10 years you've become the most successful and well-known Canadian director of your generation. Has that success affected the way you look at the world?

Well, I *do* look at the world, which I wouldn't have thought I'd be doing 10 years ago. It's interesting. Travelling with these films, you understand the incredible power of a film to transport itself to many different cultures and have a number of different effects, depending on the climate of the place where you're showing it. Also the luxury of film existing as a permanent document of a time. For example, *Family Viewing* was just released in Greece last month, after *Exotica* and *Adjuster*. The pattern of releases from *Adjuster* to *Exotica* then back to *Family Viewing* gives that particular audience a whole different take on my work, as opposed to a Canadian audience which saw *Family Viewing* first, didn't really know what to make of it and has gradually grown accustomed to my vision in a more incremental way.

Because of the travelling, you don't feel as marginalized, because you understand that in every country in the world, there's going to be a public, no matter how small, for your film. That makes creating imaginary audiences much easier, and I think any filmmaker has to create imaginary audiences. If I had to see my work as just a product of this particular milieu, it would've radically changed the shape of what I'm doing. So I'm really grateful for the fact that my films have gotten out there. From a very early point I was able to travel with them and I was able to get a sense of other responses. Though it's also *really* gratifying to see the success of *Exotica* here in Canada now. Perhaps it's a bit sweeter because it's taken so long to come about.

I'd like to talk about that in detail in just a couple of minutes, but I'd like to hear more about your feelings about success.

I'm avoiding part of this question because I see myself as the product of a group of filmmakers who were making films together at a certain point. I don't get anything from seeing myself as the leading figure of a group. Yet there's a side of me which has tried very hard to establish myself within this country. A lot of my output comes from a driving conviction that I'd prove to my own public that I had something to say. The stakes are pretty high for any person working in a mass medium, because the reward for something that's embraced publicly is pretty obvious: people go and see it. For a long time a lot of interest was generated in my work, yet at the other end, not a lot of people went to see it. That's difficult to deal with when you have this imaginary audience in your mind. So the success of *Exotica* has been gratifying though unexpected. But gratifying.

How do you account for it, then? What's happened with this film?

I think what's happened is that people are able to identify the characters more easily. They're able to trust the patterns of behaviour and to lose themselves in the world the film creates in a way they haven't been able to before. Is that because they've had a preconception of my movies that's somehow been reinforced? Or because this one conforms to some genre that they understand the film to be a part of? I'm not quite sure about that. But something makes people feel part of the movie as opposed to feeling outside of it. As opposed to feeling stupid. I think a lot of the other movies made people feel stupid because they didn't get them. And there's nothing more infuriating for a viewer than being outside of something.

It was really frustrating to me because I never wanted to exclude anyone. I'm not an academic. I'm not even able to refer to my work in a theoretical context. The reasons I make them are really emotionally loaded. Yet it's difficult to talk about those emotional links because they seem so simple and obvious, yet that's what people want to address. That's what they want to talk about. So I've had to reconcile myself to the fact that I've been branded as being an intellectual even though I know that's not the tradition I'm coming from. *Exotica*'s the first film where people are able to apprehend the structure at an intellectual level and engage in the emotional world of the film at the same time. I mean a larger audience. There have been people who've been able to do that before, but this is the film that seems to elicit that response most readily. I don't know why. What's scary is that you get used to that. In terms of my next film, I can't afford to think, 'How do I duplicate what I've already achieved?'

Another important aspect of *Exotica* is the sense of spectacle. There *is* a show you're getting. You are invited into this incredible club, and you're taken to a world that you wouldn't normally see, and that journey is really sensual. There's something pleasurable about that. You can't deny that aspect of the film. As superficial as those qualities may be, they're the things people enter in order to get to the meat of the film.

That starts with the title maybe. It's funny, because if I look at my first concepts of how the film would be marketed, they're laughable because they're a denial of what the movie's about. It's almost as though when I saw the finished film, I wanted to react against the most obvious pleasure of watching it. The real breakthrough was when the French distributor came up with this visual concept for the poster which broke through a lot of the things I wasn't prepared to admit.

You mean the design with the woman's torso framing Mia Kirshner's face?

Yeah. There are expectations this film provides which—even if they're not the ones met in the screening room—if properly engineered could bring people to the theatre. That was well done by the distributors. Hopefully that's how the film will continue to be marketed in the States. Without pandering to the most prurient aspects of the film, there's a way of generating a level of excitement about what you're going to see.

How frustrating was it for you in the past when people said they just didn't get what you were trying to do?

It was frustrating when people told me it was too cold.
You got that all the time, didn't you?
Like *all* the time. That's the thing I don't get. To me, the films are almost operatic. They're almost embarrassingly emotional. To me, there's nothing more vulnerable than showing people who are obviously trying to hold back an emotional agenda. You're really seeing the most beleaguered aspect of human dignity when someone is trying to deny what they're made up of. I thought the other films are pretty obvious in their representation of people incapable of dealing with what's on their emotional plate. But I guess not. For some people it was too out there. I just didn't know how to respond to that. You can't tell someone who says your work is cold and unfeeling that it's the opposite. So you just deal with that.

But it's been an odd apprenticeship. The first film was emotionally bare for reasons I didn't want it to be. There are a lot of devices in *Next of Kin* which were meant to pull the audience back but in fact sucked the audience right in. The whole use of hand-held camera in that film was so misconceived from what I really wanted it to do, which was to give a sense of someone watching this family trying to construct itself. But because of my lack of documentary background, what I didn't understand was, the moment you have a shaky camera you say, 'Hey this is really happening! Get right in there!' I was really thrown by a lot of the public response to *Next of Kin*, which I toured quite extensively all around Canada. Going to some of these communities and seeing how immediately people responded to something I didn't intend was horrifying.

What happened, starting with *Family Viewing*, was that I pulled back and said, 'Okay, if I have to make the formal plan really obvious in order to stake my terms, so be it.' Then I started this investigation of the film texture in a much more controlled way. That reached its peak with *The Adjuster*, which I now look at and kind of gasp at because it has reduced emotions to *such* a degree. I mean, these people are so gone, so beyond the point of return, it becomes absurd. A lot of the humour of the film is the result of how far gone these people are. They're all on the verge of suicide. If they can even muster *that* amount of emotional response.

So when I got to that extreme, I got the fortune of making a film like *Calendar* which just allowed me to do something completely untethered and spontaneous. That's pulled me back to something that I was scared of before, which is the freedom of the camera, the freedom of a filmed moment. Maybe a pulling back to what the first film was doing. I'm not sure. These things aren't calculated, but I see them now.

It's a dangerous time to talk, because I'm in a position which I haven't been in in my whole life. Which is that I haven't written anything for a year and a half, since the birth of Arshile. I haven't really been involved in something intensively, so it's given me a perspective which I wanted but I'm a bit frightened about, because a lot of things seemed really clear to me. I've also been doing a lot of retrospectives, which are dangerous things at the best of times. The best example is in Woody Allen's *Stardust Memories,* where this guy is kind of tortured into watching all his own films.

In Glasgow about a year ago, they screened all my films back to back at this theatre, and I just arrived in time with Arsinée and Arshile. *Calendar,* which was the latest film, was just finishing. Just walking into this room you could feel what people had been through for the past seven hours! Then having to deal with this in this kind of conversation, these questions and answers. It's dangerous to have that much perspective over what you're doing, but it's been unavoidable.

Maybe that's why I'm drawn now to working with someone else's material, because I've lost a rhythm I've carefully maintained since the age of 14 when I began writing plays.

Is audience an idea that figures prominently in your creative process?

An imaginary audience, definitely. But it's not any real audience. An imaginary audience that gets everything you want to convey is very important. It's a conversation with yourself ultimately. It's not the type of audience you would test-market a film with. But yes, I'm constantly playing my films to dream viewers, because a lot of the energy of the film is dependent on the process of self-consciously viewing my movies, what the process of viewing them actually means. There's a strange chemistry that happens between the act of my committing these images to film and someone then self-consciously watching them on a screen. So I have to be aware of what the other side of that process means. What it is the viewer expects to happen or see, and how I'm either playing against that or playing into it.

I mean, you don't write a scene with Francis driving Tracey home the first time, dropping her off, exchanging money with her, and not think about the audience believing this is a child prostitute. You have to be aware of that or you're just being coy. You're having fun with that too.

Why does the Canadian success of Exotica *mean so much to you? Lots of people would say, 'Atom, they love you in Europe, so who cares?'*

I see my films as being set in a particular society. The response of that society to the work, and the recognition of themselves through the work, and the pleasure and the catharsis and the dialogue that's created through that process, is something I've always romanticized and never had the luxury of seeing realized. So it's really gratifying to have that. So many different types of people are seeing this film now. It's just touched on a lot of things that are really interesting to, well, Torontonians, to start with, particularly in terms of the whole table-dancing phenomenon.

I can't really be specific. I *know* the films are set in Toronto. They couldn't be set anywhere else. I know that every time I go back west, because I was raised in Victoria, and it's so funny to see how the Vancouver press see me as being a western boy, and one side of me definitely is. But I couldn't set my films in any other city but Toronto. I don't even know if I could say why exactly, I just know that. To me there's something essentially funny about a can-do mentality with dysfunctional people. 'We'll carry on, it's business as usual, but we're very disturbed. Things are definitely not right at home, but we'll still come to audit your business, we'll still adjust your claims. We'll still do whatever it is we have to do to keep the social apparatus going.' And the fact that no one even limps is something I find touching yet very Torontonian.

So that hometown recognition has finally come with Exotica.

Yeah. I'm not sure it's come for the right reasons. There's a part of me that doesn't want to accept the fact that there is, as I'll call it at this point, the 'David Gilmour factor.' I didn't see the show, but apparently in his year-end round-up on CBC's 'Prime Time News', he said this was one of his top five films because it was made by a guy who obviously loves women. There's bound to be that sexual aspect to it, but I don't think that's the prevailing reason people like it. Like we've said before, the fact that people trust the film has been immensely rewarding because it means that people know when to take me seriously but also … I don't know. You begin to sound pretentious when you talk about the reasons why it means a lot to you. I'm still at a relatively early point in my career, so I'm not going to say that I've been working years towards this, but in a way I have. Still, lot of people have been working a lot harder for a longer period of time.

You recently took home a number of Genie awards from the Academy of Canadian Film and Television, awards that had, until that point, eluded you. Did the industry recognition matter to you as well?

I didn't realize how significant the Genies were until I actually got up to accept the award. I looked out at the audience and realized that those were people who actually nominated and selected the film. I've always really felt somehow outside the industry. I always felt that people were resentful of the reputation I had, and suddenly that evening I felt as though there had been a coming to terms, I suppose.

I feel very uncomfortable about all this stuff, because for so long I've gotten a certain energy from being outside that it's difficult for me to accept the fact that part of me has now been accepted into the system. But of course it completely has. The moment you make a film that as many people have gone to see as *Exotica*, or has been as awarded by the industry as *Exotica*, you've been absorbed by the system. So anyone who's defined themselves outside of it can't help but feel a bit uncomfortable. But that's happened, and I don't feel I've compromised anything in order to allow it to happen.

Do you see yourself as fitting into any kind of a Canadian tradition?

We're still defining all our traditions, so it's dangerous to say that you fit into a tradition that you were part of the evolution of. I do think that a new generation of filmmakers were introduced with the demise of the tax-shelter movies in the early '80s. Those talents are finding their way and I'm part of that tradition.

I definitely feel part of a community and I definitely feel part of a critical community. I can't help but think of you and people like you as being part of the same tradition that I'm evolving within. It's hard to talk about these things. These are the type of issues that are probably easier for you to address because you've seen so many of the films.

I realize that the whole issue of traditions in something as open-ended and still evolving as Canadian film is tricky, but I was curious to ask you anyway. Let me try something else. How do you think your approach to working with actors has changed over the years?

I don't think it's changed as much as it's become less insecure. I used to think that as a director, you had to go into the relationship with all the answers in place. I used to approach the process of rehearsal as one where I had to do a tremendous amount of homework to make sure that there were no holes in the motivations or in the logical development of the characters that I'd drawn out. But now I understand that there are things that'll be explored and defined by the relationship you have with the actor, and that you don't have to feel as guarded or defensive. I don't think I was defensive, but I was consumed with the idea of design. At the beginning, all the films were storyboarded down to the frame. In the same way, all the actors' gestures and ways of moving were carefully plotted out. I didn't really allow for a lot of spontaneity.

Something very important happened with *Exotica* which is worth retelling. It has to do with the character of Eric. I presented the script to Elias [Koteas] and he was really excited about it. There was some discussion from various sources that his monologues were too extreme. This whole idea of talking about 'What is it about a young girl that gives her this special charm?' and his talking about her smell. Some people got very worried about that. At the time, because of various other pressures I was facing, I thought, 'Okay, that's easy enough to change,' and I just toned down the speeches. I got back this call from Elias where he said, 'You've just completely taken out what was most interesting about this character. How can you do that?' It kind of shocked me into a recognition of the fact that he was able to be far more protective of this person than I ever could. It was really dependent on the actor to defend that character, even to the person who created the character! That was an important moment for me, a real breakthrough.

I've certainly experienced that in my relationship with Arsinée [Khanjian]. She's very, very demanding of what her characters have to be. But I've always thought that was a privilege of our relationship. To invite other actors to have the same defensive measures as she had about protecting who they had to portray is a license I now look forward to giving other actors.

I've just been lucky in being able to work with really intelligent actors. They've all been people who've been able to trust and understand the many different levels their characters would have. But sometimes in that process, because the characters had transformed themselves into archetypes or parodies of themselves in order to deal with the psychological issues in front of them, the actors may have been hesitant to address really basic human concerns. That's evolving, I think.

Tell me about the casting of Exotica. *How many people were there, like Elias, that you had really preselected for parts?*

I don't cast a very wide net with my movies. The thing that's unusual about the films is that I haven't used a casting director up until this point. That might change now.

You've never used one?

Never have. I've always cast them myself and I've always cast based on people I've seen in theatre or other films. The problem with that is I'm not going to find someone who surprises me because they're outside of what I expected, which is what a good casting director does. I have a pretty clear idea of the type of person I want to work with, and it's a matter of seeing who will best serve that. Casting is probably the least adventurous part of the whole process for me. Maybe that's something that has to change. On the other hand, I've been really happy with the performances I've got and the chemistry I've had. I think it's because as a writer-director I have the luxury of imagining people in the parts as I'm writing them, and I take advantage of that.

A really unusual choice, it strikes me, for Exotica *was Bruce Greenwood, a Canadian actor best known for work on American TV. How did you settle on him for Francis?*

An odd way. At one point I was thinking—and you can't think of someone more completely different from Bruce than Maury Chaykin—but Maury was one of the people I was thinking of for Francis.

That sure would've been a different film.

Totally different. But the schedule with Maury didn't work out so Maury's agent, Debbie Peck, suggested Bruce, and I owe a lot to her. At the moment I saw Bruce's work I thought he'd be perfect, because I love the idea of a man being found in a club like that whom you wouldn't think would need to be there. It immediately makes you wonder why he's been brought there.

I rely on a few casting agents in this city whom I've worked with a lot over the past few years, and I must confess that I work within a pretty small circle. But that'll open up when I get a casting director. The problem with the way I make my movies is that I've fallen into certain patterns. There are certain things I've been doing myself for so long that it's difficult to relinquish those positions. To me, they're part of what goes into making the film. But at a certain point that becomes cumbersome and you just have to realize that you're being silly and far too conservative.

Any dream people you'd like to cast?

Yeah, of course. I'm fascinated by Christopher Walken. I just can't take my eyes off him. I'm always fascinated by Vanessa Redgrave as well. I really like Clint Eastwood. It was kind of odd when he was on the jury in Cannes when *Exotica* was in competition. It was one of the few times when someone saw a movie of mine and I really wanted to be beside that person as they were watching it. But I guess he didn't like it that much. The French actor Philippe Noiret is someone I really like. I wish he could speak English because I'd love to work with him. Donald Sutherland. I don't know. I can never answer questions like this.

I'm not sure you'll like this one any more. A few months ago, in a national

EXOTICA

weekly newsmagazine, a full-page picture appeared of you and Arsinée and your son Arshile. Since Arsinée has figured so prominently in your films, your relationship has developed a public as well as private dimension. How do you feel about your private life becoming part of the publicity package of your own career?

I'm uncomfortable about it, but it's a given. There's no turning back. Once *Calendar* was released and people started asking me if Arsinée and I had actually broken up, I realized in a strange way that our relationship is part of the alchemy of the films themselves. That's dangerous as hell and I understand that. But at this point, to turn off those valves would be naïve and create sort of an event in itself. I'm really envious of people who are able to separate their personal lives from their professional ones, but there's no mistaking the fact that these films are intensely personal and I'm offering myself up for scrutiny as I make them, so my lifestyle is also subject to observation.

It goes back to the point in this interview when I started proclaiming how normal my sexuality is. What an odd thing for me to have to say! But I'm so used to being in that situation that it's second nature. It's also odd that what I've been defending for so long—that adolescent relationship I mentioned that was the motivation to make *Exotica*—I feel I can now talk about because I'll be beyond the publicity blitz by the time this gets published. I *won't* talk about it with the American release, which is coming up. But this will be published well after the launch and the sound-bite phase. So it's a question of measuring it and it's a question of trying to understand how you've made an artifact of your relationship.

It's a personal thing we have to deal with in terms of the difference between the people we appear to be to others, and who we understand ourselves to be to each other. As long as we're able to make that delineation, it's a bit safer. The problem is when you involve a child in it. That's where we have to be very careful. But I think we're just going to feel our way through that. At this point it would be more artificial to exclude Arshile from our lives than to have included him the way we have in the travelling and the promotion of the film. It would be more painful to separate him because he's just a really well-adjusted kid. Maybe he's going to end up being a psychopath—I pray to God not—but right now he seems very socially adept and well adjusted because he's constantly with us. It would take more effort and be more strenuous to separate him from us than to include him.

And I think it's important that he knows what we do. One of the things I really value about my upbringing is that I always knew what my father did. I don't want to mystify what we do to our child. And part of what we do is open aspects of our lives to scrutiny. Arshile can reject that, and probably will, but I think it's important that he understand who his parents are.

Your first 10 years making movies has, I would imagine, been pretty adventurous, fulfilling and successful. How would you like to see the next decade unfold?

I'd like it to be more measured. I'd like to spend more time developing the scripts and not feeling that I have to pour the stuff out as much. First of all, as I said before, I don't think I can, and secondly, I've reached a point where I want to access other people's visions and try and incorporate that into my work as part of its evolution. To nourish, I guess, my vision of things. The things that I've been drawing from for the past 10 years are basically the literature and theatre and film I saw in my late adolescence and early 20s. That continues to be very inspiring to me, but it's time to make myself more aware of other influences.

But you're asking me at a time when I'm being much more reflective than I usually am. Maybe the next script will be one of my own. I don't know. It's difficult to say.

EXOTICA

Alliance Communications Corporation presents An Ego Film Arts Production Produced with the participation of Telefilm Canada and the Ontario Film Development Corporation.

Writer/Director/Producer Atom Egoyan
Producer Camelia Frieberg
Associate Producer David Webb
Director of Photography Paul Sarossy
Production Designers Linda Del Rosario, Richard Paris
Costume Designer Linda Muir
Editor Susan Shipton
Sound Designer Steven Munro
Music Mychael Danna

Starring (in order of appearance)
Customs Inspector David Hemblen
Customs Officer (Ian) Calvin Green
Thomas Don McKellar
Man in Taxi Peter Krantz
Christina Mia Kirshner
Zoe Arsinée Khanjian
Eric Elias Koteas
Francis Bruce Greenwood
Man at opera #1 Damon d'Oliveira
Tracey Sarah Polley
Harold Victor Garber
Scalper Jack Blum
Man at opera #2 Billy Merasty
Doorman Ken McDougall

EXOTICA

1. Title credits.
Over a shot of the interior of the strip club Exotica.

>   CUSTOMS INSPECTOR
>   *(voice-over)*
>   You have to ask yourself what
>   brought the person to this point.
>   What was seen in his face, his man-
>   ner, that channelled him here ...

2. Interior. Airport. Customs office. Night.
Behind a one-way mirror, THOMAS *is being watched by two inspectors. One customs officer is training a new employee,* IAN.

>   CUSTOMS INSPECTOR
>   ... You have to convince yourself that
>   this person has something hidden
>   that you have to find. You check his
>   bags, but it's his face, his gestures,
>   that you are really watching ...

3. Interior. Airport. Customs. Night.
On the other side of the mirror, THOMAS *is having his bags inspected.*

>   CUSTOMS INSP. #2
>   Thank you.

THOMAS *walks towards the mirror and stares at his reflection.*

EXOTICA

4. **Interior. Airport. Customs. Night.**

   By coincidence, THOMAS *is also staring directly at the face of* IAN *on the other side of the mirror.*

   > CUSTOMS INSPECTOR
   > He's staring straight at you. Look at him carefully. What do you see?

5. **Exterior. Airport. Night.**

   THOMAS *watches as his luggage is placed in the trunk of a cab. He is approached by a businessman.*

   > MAN IN TAXI
   > Which way are you headed?

   > THOMAS
   > Downtown.

   > MAN IN TAXI
   > Do you want to split it?

   > THOMAS
   > Sure.

6. **Interior/Exterior. Taxi. Travelling. Night.**

   THOMAS *is feeling something hidden under his shirt. The businessman talks on his cellular phone.*

   > MAN IN TAXI
   > What? Not tonight. Are you sure?
   > Well, can't you cancel?

   The businessman gets out of the cab at his destination and hands THOMAS *an envelope.*

   > THOMAS
   > Oh. What are these?

   > MAN IN TAXI
   > Ballet tickets for tonight.

                    THOMAS
        Oh.

                    MAN IN TAXI
        You don't like ballet?

                    THOMAS
        Well, some ballets.

                    MAN IN TAXI
        Well that's exactly what this is. Some
        ballet. Look, you can always scalp the
        tickets at the door.

                    THOMAS
        Oh, you mean take these in exchange
        for you paying your part of the fare.

                    MAN IN TAXI
        Well, what did you think?

The cab pulls away revealing a woman walking along the street. CHRISTINA *walks into a nightclub called Exotica.*

7. **Interior. Exotica. Night.**
CHRISTINA *walks down the hallway towards the pulsating music. She enters Exotica, an exclusive, high-concept strip palace. The club is full of table dancers and there is a central stage where the women perform. The atmosphere is steamy, charged and intoxicating. As* CHRISTINA *makes her way to the dressing room she is greeted by the club's owner,* ZOE, *an attractive woman in her 30s who is seven months pregnant. Throughout the film,* ZOE *wears various wigs and colourful robes.*

                    ZOE
        Christina, there you are. People are
        asking for you.

The camera pans up to the emcee's booth to reveal ERIC.

EXOTICA

Screenplay

> ERIC
> Yeah. Let's bring those big hairy palms together gentlemen, and have a big round of applause for Kali. Yes indeed, Kali. You too can have Kali come over to your table for only $5 and she can show you the mysteries of her world. Trust me gentlemen, trust me.

8. **Interior. Thomas's apartment. Night.**

THOMAS *is carefully unwrapping some tape he has wrapped around his midriff. He winces as he peels the tape off. Hidden under the tape are rare eggs that* THOMAS *has smuggled into the country. He inspects the eggs carefully. After getting ready for the ballet, he checks on the eggs—which are now in an incubator— and checks his watch.*

9. **Interior. Exotica. Night.**

ERIC *introduces* CHRISTINA.

> ERIC
> Awww, baby, baby, baby. Do it for me baby. My God, that's incredible! Let me ask you something, gentlemen. What is it that gives a schoolgirl her special innocence? Her sweet fragrance? Fresh flowers? Light spring rain? Oh my God, my God. Or is it her firm, young flesh inviting your every caress, enticing you to explore the deepest, most private secrets? Well gentlemen, I'm going to let you decide that one for yourselves. Please join me in welcoming a sassy bit of jailbait to our stage. Yes indeed. Come out sweet Chrissy. Wherever you are baby, come on out.

An interplay of looks takes place between ERIC *and* ZOE *for the last few lines of* ERIC*'s introduction.*

Angle on CHRISTINA *as she comes onto the stage. She is wearing a plaid schoolgirl's skirt, a white blouse and a tie. She carries a leather schoolbag, which she places on the stage. She dances to Leonard Cohen's 'Everybody Knows.'*

10. **Exterior. Opera house. Night.**
'Everybody Knows' *continues as* THOMAS *moves through a crowd towards the opera house.*

11. **Interior. Exotica. Night.**
'Everybody Knows' *continues.* CHRISTINA *continues her dance.* ERIC *watches.*

> ERIC
> You think you're bad, baby? You're bad.

A man, FRANCIS, *also watches* CHRISTINA *like a hawk.*

12. **Exterior. Opera house. Night.**
THOMAS *continues walking through the crowd outside. There are students standing about with signs, looking for tickets.* THOMAS *stares at the choice of who to share his tickets with. His eyes fall upon an extremely attractive young man. (His sign reads: One ticket please.)*

13. **Interior. Opera house. Night.**
THOMAS *sits with the man he saw outside. He steals a sidelong stare at the young man's crotch. The man catches* THOMAS*'s look but does not let on.*

14. **Interior. Exotica. Night.**
CHRISTINA *sits/dances for* FRANCIS. *They talk and she moves seductively towards him.* ERIC *watches from behind a one-way mirror in a secret observation hallway.* ERIC *is holding his emcee microphone.* ZOE *comes into the hallway.*

15. **Interior. Exotica. Hallway. Night.**

> ZOE
> Eric?

> ERIC
> What?

EXOTICA

ERIC
Linda finished her dance ...

ERIC *realizes he has missed his cue and begins talking into the microphone, his gaze still fixed upon* CHRISTINA. *He walks up towards his emcee booth to entice the men into buying table dances.*

ERIC
Let's bring those big hairy palms together, gentlemen. Yeah, gentlemen. Yes. Let's have a nice big round of applause for Linda. Yes indeed, Linda. And just to remind you, there is nothing Linda would love more than to slink over to your table and give you your own private show for only $5. That's right. Five dollars is all that it takes to have one of our beautiful foxes come over to your table and get you all hot and bothered. But hey, why be bothered when you're being treated like a king? You've had a rough day. Don't you think you owe it to yourself to do something that'll make you feel like you're someone special? You are someone special. Five dollars is all it takes to prove it.

CHRISTINA *continues to dance for* FRANCIS. ERIC *stares at her.* FRANCIS *gets up and leaves.* ERIC *continues announcing ...*

ERIC
Let's have a nice big round of applause for Michelle. My God, that was beautiful. Oh, baby, you come on out. Just to remind you that there is nothing Michelle would love more than to come over to your table and give you your own private dance. HELLO gentlemen ...

16. Interior. Exotica. Washroom. Night.

FRANCIS *goes into a stall in the washroom.* ERIC's *voice is heard over.*

> ERIC
> Anybody out there? Anybody alive?
> For just $5 you could have Kali at
> your own private table.

17. Interior. Exotica. Night.

Camera angles on ERIC *as he introduces* CHRISTINA. *A play of looks takes place between* ERIC *and* CHRISTINA.

> ERIC
> Let me ask you something gentle-
> men. What is it about a schoolgirl
> that gives her her special innocence?
> Is it the way that they gaze at you?
> Waiting for you to say something with
> so much expectation and hope that
> you're paralyzed into ... into silence.

18. Exterior. Field. Day.

An empty field in summer. People begin to slowly appear, walking over a large distant hill.

19. Interior. Exotica. Washroom. Night.

FRANCIS *is sitting in a washroom stall. He takes a few deep breaths.*

20. Exterior. Opera house. Night.

The ballet is over. THOMAS *hands the young man his money back.*

> THOMAS
> Look, I want to give this back to you.

> MAN AT OPERA #1
> Why?

> THOMAS
> Well, those tickets were given to me,

and I just feel uncomfortable about having sold them.

            MAN AT OPERA #1
That's okay.

            THOMAS
No, no, really. We never really introduced ourselves. I'm Thomas.

            MAN AT OPERA #1
David. Can I use this to take you out for a drink?

            THOMAS
Oh, well that's very kind of you but ...

            MAN AT OPERA #1
But what?

            THOMAS
But I really have to get home.

21. Exterior. Harold/Tracey's apartment. Night.
It is a rough area of town. Hip-hop plays and people loiter outside a Roti shop in a mini-plaza. A car, FRANCIS's *car, pulls into a parking lot.* FRANCIS *and* TRACEY *are in the car.* TRACEY *is listening to music through headphones.* FRANCIS *hands her some money.*

            TRACEY
Thanks.

            FRANCIS
Are you available next Thursday?

            TRACEY
I think so, yeah.

            FRANCIS
Good. Tracey?

TRACEY
Yeah?

FRANCIS
I'm not that boring, am I?

TRACEY
What do you mean?

FRANCIS
Well. The earphones. We used to listen to the radio and you used to ask me all sorts of questions.

TRACEY
So you want me to ask more questions?

FRANCIS
Sure. If there's something you want to know.

TRACEY
Okay, I'll see what I can think up.

FRANCIS
Say hi to your dad.

TRACEY
I will. Goodnight.

FRANCIS
Goodnight.

TRACEY *gets out of the car and walks to the apartment door.* FRANCIS *watches from the car until she closes the door behind her.*

22. Interior. Exotica. Zoe's office. Night.
ERIC *and* ZOE *are in her office having a discussion.* ZOE *has taken off her wigs and her costumes.*

ERIC
Did someone say something?

ZOE
No.

ERIC
So what's the point?

ZOE
I've just noticed a change in your attitude ... Look, I would understand if you would prefer not to introduce Christina. I could do it myself. Actually I've been thinking that perhaps I should be getting more involved in the introductions overall. I could have my own microphone like my mother used to do.

ERIC
No, I actually enjoy introducing Christina. I find it very therapeutic, you know.

ZOE
That's not what you're getting paid for.

ERIC
Well, it seems to me that I'm being paid to make every girl seem like she's something special. So, in order to do that, I have to let my imagination run wild. So when it comes to Christina, my imagination is bound to run a little wilder. There's nothing I can do to control that, Zoe.

ZOE
It makes the clients uncomfortable.

ERIC
And you think your state puts them at ease?

ERIC *looks at* ZOE's *pregnant belly.*

ERIC
Is he kicking?

ZOE
All the time ... Do you feel like touching it?

ERIC *walks over towards her and feels* ZOE's *belly.*

ZOE
How are you feeling about this?

ERIC
Fine.

ZOE
Fine? Are you happy?

ERIC
For you.

ZOE
What about you, Eric? What about you?

ERIC
Well, I guess I have to be pretty careful about my feelings, right? I mean, that's why we have a contract, isn't it?

EXOTICA

23. Interior. Pet store. Day.

'Bird of Paradise' is THOMAS's *store. It is a pet store specializing in exotic animals. It seems run down, the aquariums are murky and dirty and most of the bird cages are empty.* THOMAS *is on the phone having an argument.*

> THOMAS
>
> There's plaster dust all over the apartment. No, I'm not exaggerating. I was coughing in my sleep last night. You told me it was going to be comfortable for me to live there. And it is not comfortable. There's plastic on the furniture, that is not comfortable living. Oh, come on, look, you told me you were going to strip the wallpaper, not strip the walls down. Well, if you'd told me in the first place, if you'd told me what kind of job it was, then I would have considered it. Although it makes it seem like you maybe made a mistake ...

FRANCIS *walks into the pet store, briefcase in hand.* THOMAS *continues his argument.*

> THOMAS
>
> ... that's what it makes me suspect. No, it's too late now, it's inaccessible. I am not going to pay you! Pay you for what? You didn't do the job. Well, you did a job, but it's not the job that I asked you to do, it's not the job we agreed on. I can get anyone, any number of people to do this. Yes, that's just fine with me.

FRANCIS *has made his way over to one of the bird cages with a bird in it. He watches the bird while* THOMAS *finishes his conversation and hangs up.*

THOMAS
Yes, can I help you?

FRANCIS *straightens and turns towards* THOMAS.

FRANCIS
Mr. Pinto?

THOMAS
Yes.

FRANCIS
I'm Francis Brown. We spoke on the phone a couple of weeks ago. Revenue Canada.

THOMAS
Yes, of course.

FRANCIS
How was your trip?

THOMAS
Fine.

FRANCIS
When did you get back?

THOMAS
Just yesterday.

The phone begins to ring.

FRANCIS
Good weather?

THOMAS
Yes. Lovely.

FRANCIS
Is this a good time, Mr. Pinto?

THOMAS
Sure.

FRANCIS
It's just you seem a little ...

THOMAS
A little what?

FRANCIS
Flustered.

THOMAS
Oh, no, no, no. I'm fine. *(he points Francis in the direction of the back office and goes to answer the phone)* Yeah, yeah, I can't talk to you right now. Later.

They walk to the back of the pet store and THOMAS *opens up some filing cabinets for* FRANCIS.

FRANCIS
So, this is where I'd find all the bank statements?

THOMAS
That's right, and those there.

FRANCIS
Okay. Well, if I have any questions, I'll let you know.

THOMAS
Is it a little hot for you back here?

FRANCIS
Yes. You could turn it down a tad. I suppose you have to be really careful with the temperature with the animals.

THOMAS
Oh, well, they're a lot hardier than you think.

FRANCIS
I wouldn't think that they're not hardy. Just because they're exotic doesn't mean they can't endure extremes. It is, after all, a jungle out there, isn't it?

THOMAS
So, how long will this take?

FRANCIS
An audit? Well, it depends on how prepared you are. Do you have an accountant?

THOMAS
Well, not really, no.

FRANCIS
Not really.

THOMAS
So this will take a while?

FRANCIS
I could be done by the end of the day. Or it might take a week. It's difficult to say.

EXOTICA

> THOMAS
> Oh, okay. Well, if you have any questions ...

> FRANCIS
> I'll let you know.

24. Exterior. Field. Day

It is two years earlier. CHRISTINA, ERIC *and a number of other people walk through the field. They are searching for something.*

> ERIC
> Did you know her?

> CHRISTINA
> Sort of.

> ERIC
> She was your neighbour?

> CHRISTINA
> I babysat her a couple of times.

> ERIC
> Oh, so you knew her pretty well, eh?

> CHRISTINA
> Yeah, I did. What about you?

> ERIC
> Oh, I just heard this thing was being organized so I ... It seems so surreal, doesn't it?

> CHRISTINA
> What?

> ERIC
> That we'd find anything. There's so

many places you could hide something in this country.

25. Interior. Exotica. Zoe's office. Day.

CHRISTINA *looks into a cupboard. The voices of the previous conversation are heard over.*

ERIC

My name is Eric.

CHRISTINA

I'm Christina.

ERIC

Nice to meet you, Christina.

CHRISTINA *shuts the door, revealing* ZOE *in the background feeling her stomach.* CHRISTINA *walks towards her, watching her.*

ZOE

Well?

CHRISTINA

Well what?

ZOE

Well, don't you want to touch it? You don't have to. It's one of those things people normally like to do.

CHRISTINA *kneels in front of* ZOE *and lifts up her shirt, pulls her waistband down to reveal* ZOE's *pregnant stomach. She begins to feel* ZOE's *stomach.*

ZOE

What is this thing about Eric calling you a sassy piece of jailbait?

CHRISTINA

What's this thing?

EXOTICA

> ZOE
> It bothers me.

> CHRISTINA
> Why?

> ZOE
> It makes you out like a child or something.

> CHRISTINA
> Unlike the tartan skirt, my socks, my blouse or the way I act, right?

> ZOE
> Do you find it strange that he would still want to work here?

> CHRISTINA
> Zoe, not all of us have the luxury of deciding what to do with our lives. It's a job and he's getting paid all right.

> ZOE
> I just find it cruel.

> CHRISTINA
> So fire him. As a favour.

> ZOE
> How can you be so detached?

ZOE *leans in towards* CHRISTINA *who meets her for a kiss.*

26. **Interior. Pet store. Office. Day.**
FRANCIS *is still in the back room punching numbers into a calculator and writing in a ledger. He is startled by the sound of a large fish in the tank in front of him. When his pen runs out, he begins searching for one in* THOMAS's *desk. What he finds instead is a hand gun.*

27. Interior. Pet store. Front room. Day.

FRANCIS *is leaving for the day, carrying his briefcase.* THOMAS *is fixing a leak in a fish tank in the front of the store.*

FRANCIS
Well, I'm finished for the day.

THOMAS
For the day? You mean you have to come back.

FRANCIS
I'm afraid so. When is a good time?

THOMAS
But I thought you said it was only going to take one day.

FRANCIS
Well, it can only take a day. But you have to understand that you don't keep very well-organized books. That's why you should really think about getting someone in to help you. Just someone to come in once or twice a week, depending on the amount of activity, and the type of activity …

THOMAS
What do you mean by that?

FRANCIS
Well, some types of activity are more complicated, aren't they? It might take more effort to account for.

THOMAS
Oh.

FRANCIS
I found a gun in one of the drawers.

THOMAS
Oh, that belonged to my dad.

FRANCIS
Your dad?

THOMAS
Yeah, I guess he just kept it just in case.

FRANCIS
In case of what?

THOMAS
Well, in case of trouble.

FRANCIS
With the animals? Would Monday be a good time for me to come back, Mr. Pinto?

THOMAS
How about tomorrow?

FRANCIS *begins walking towards the door.*

FRANCIS
I have appointments for tomorrow. Actually, I'm pretty busy until the end of the week. Monday's not good?

THOMAS
No, Monday's fine.

FRANCIS
Around ten?

> THOMAS
> Yeah, sure.

> FRANCIS
> Well good. Have a nice weekend.

28. Exterior. Harold/Tracey's apartment. Day.
HAROLD *and* FRANCIS *are on the balcony waiting for* TRACEY *to come home.* HAROLD *is in a wheelchair, and has a parrot sitting on his shoulder. There is much tension between the two men.*

> FRANCIS
> Strange to think that that bird is probably going to outlive us.

> HAROLD
> Strange?

> FRANCIS
> Did you ever teach it to say anything?

> HAROLD
> Yes.

> FRANCIS
> What does it say, Harold?

> HAROLD
> Well, it doesn't really say it any more.

> FRANCIS
> It forgot?

> HAROLD
> I don't think so. They're not supposed to forget. It must have just lost interest.

TRACEY *walks out onto the balcony.*

> TRACEY
> Sorry I'm late.

> FRANCIS
> It's okay. We were just talking about Felix.

> TRACEY
> What about him? Dad?

> FRANCIS
> I had the piano tuned. It sounds beautiful.

29. Interior. Francis's house. Dusk.

FRANCIS *comes down the stairs and into the living room where* TRACEY *is playing the piano. It is a beautiful baby grand.*

> FRANCIS
> So, how does it sound?

> TRACEY
> Good.

> FRANCIS
> Yeah? Good. Well, I shouldn't be too late.

> TRACEY
> What's too late?

> FRANCIS
> Around eleven or so?

> THOMAS
> Okay.

TRACEY *continues her piece.* FRANCIS *stares at the picture above the mantle before leaving. The picture is of a woman and a young girl, both smiling. The girl wears a school uniform—tartan skirt, white blouse, tie.*

30. **Exterior. Opera house. Dusk.**

THOMAS *approaches the opera house. The performance is sold out. He is approached by a scalper.*

       SCALPER
    You looking for tickets?

       THOMAS
    Yeah, how much?

31. **Exterior. Exotica. Dusk.**

FRANCIS's *car pulls into a parking lot; the skyline of the city is in the background. He locks his car and walks towards Exotica.*

32. **Exterior. Opera house. Dusk.**

THOMAS *walks through the crowd with his two scalped tickets. His eyes search the collection of people with small placards expressing their need for a ticket. As before,* THOMAS's *eyes fall upon an attractive young man holding a sign reading 'I need one ticket.'* THOMAS *holds up one ticket and smiles.*

33. **Interior. Exotica. Dusk.**

FRANCIS *walks into the club and finds a table.* CHRISTINA *is dancing for another customer.* FRANCIS *stops to watch her. She notices him and stops for a brief moment. We hear* ERIC ...

       ERIC
    He comes in here every other night.
    He has his favourite drink, at his
    favourite table, with his favourite
    dancer. Sometimes he has to wait for
    her and sometimes she's waiting for
    him. She'll protect him, she's his
    angel ...

ERIC *plugs the microphone in. We realize that he was watching* CHRISTINA *and* FRANCIS *and was talking to himself, more or less. Now he addresses everyone in Exotica.*

       ERIC
    All right ladies and gentlemen. It's

show time at Exotica. Just to remind you that $5 is all it takes to have one of our lovely ladies come over to your table and show the mysteries of their world.

34. Interior. Francis's house. Night.

TRACEY *slips a disc into a machine beside the piano and the piano begins to play by itself.* TRACEY *gets up, stands in front of a music stand and plays the flute.*

35. Interior. Exotica. Night.

The music from the previous scene continues. CHRISTINA *is on-stage doing her routine.* FRANCIS *gazes from the shadow of the club at her, watching her every move. He turns towards the mirror at his side and looks at himself. Unbeknownst to him, he is staring straight through a one-way mirror into the face of* ERIC *who stands in the hidden observation hallway.* ERIC *mimics him.*

> ERIC
> If that didn't turn you on gentlemen, nothing will. Let's have a nice big warm round of applause for Christina, gentlemen. Yes, Christina.

CHRISTINA *now dances for* FRANCIS. *She is seductive; he looks almost distraught.*

> CHRISTINA
> What are you thinking?

> FRANCIS
> I was just thinking, what would happen if someone ever hurt you?

> CHRISTINA
> How could anyone hurt me?

> FRANCIS
> If I'm not there to protect you.

CHRISTINA
You'll always be there to protect me.

Once again, ERIC *watches them like a hawk from the vantage point of his emcee booth.*

FRANCIS
An angel.

CHRISTINA
Shhhh.

FRANCIS
Why would somebody want to do something like that? How could somebody even think of doing something like that?

CHRISTINA
You mustn't worry.

ERIC *is so consumed with watching* FRANCIS *and* CHRISTINA *that he once again forgets to announce the dancers.*

ZOE
Eric! Eric!

ERIC
Ahhh, all hot and bothered. Let's have a nice big round of applause for Melinda.

36. **Interior. Exotica. Washroom. Night.**
FRANCIS *retreats into the bathroom to get ahold of himself.*

37. **Interior. Francis's house. Night.**
TRACEY *looks at the many photos of* FRANCIS*'s wife and daughter.*

Videotaped footage of the wife and daughter playing the piano, laughing and smiling.

EXOTICA

38. Interior. Exotica. Washroom. Night.

FRANCIS *in a washroom stall, breathing heavily and looking pained.*

39. Exterior. Opera house. Night.

The ballet is over. THOMAS *is once again returning the money he had previously taken from his companion.*

>THOMAS
>Listen, I feel bad about taking your money ...

>MAN AT OPERA #2
>Why?

>THOMAS
>Well, the tickets were given to me, and I should have given them away for free.

>MAN AT OPERA #2
>Well, that would have been stupid.

>THOMAS
>Why?

>MAN AT OPERA #2
>Because no one gives anything away. Are you sure?

>THOMAS
>Yes, I'm positive.

Production stills from *Exotica*: Elias Koteas as ERIC; Arsinée Khanjian as ZOE; the club Exotica; Bruce Greenwood as FRANCIS, Mia Kirshner as CHRISTINA; Mia Kirshner as CHRISTINA, Arsinée Khanjian as ZOE; Elias Koteas as ERIC; Bruce Greenwood as FRANCIS, Sarah Polley as TRACEY; Mia Kirshner as CHRISTINA, Don McKellar as THOMAS; Elias Koteas as ERIC, Bruce Greenwood as FRANCIS; Elias Koteas as ERIC, Mia Kirshner as CHRISTINA.

40. Exterior. Harold/Tracey's apartment. Night.

As before, there are people loitering around outside the mini-plaza. FRANCIS *stares at the menacing thugs hanging around outside as* TRACEY *begins to speak.*

TRACEY
Do you consider my dad a friend?

FRANCIS
Why?

TRACEY
Just asking.

FRANCIS
Does he consider me a friend?

TRACEY
I don't know.

FRANCIS
Why not?

TRACEY
Because he always seems different when you're around.

FRANCIS
Different in what way?

TRACEY
Tense.

FRANCIS
Is that bad?

TRACEY
Well, I don't really like to feel tense around my friends.

FRANCIS
Well, sure. I didn't like to feel tense around my friends when I was your age.

TRACEY
But you do now?

FRANCIS
It's not a question of liking it or not, it's just something that happens.

TRACEY
Why?

FRANCIS
Well, as you get older, you become aware that the people you meet, and the person you are, are carrying a certain amount of baggage. And that baggage creates tension.

TRACEY
So what do you do about it?

FRANCIS
Well, you can pretend that it's not there, or you can choose not to have friends, or you can acknowledge that it's there and have friends anyway.

TRACEY
Like my dad?

FRANCIS
Right.

TRACEY
I don't think that I like my dad when he's around you.

> FRANCIS
> Well, that's because your dad doesn't like himself when he's around me. But that's okay. It's part of what friends do to each other.

> TRACEY
> Goodnight.

> FRANCIS
> Goodnight.

41. Exterior. Field. Day.

FRANCIS *and* CHRISTINA *walk through the tall grass and they talk. Other people are also seen walking beside them.*

> CHRISTINA
> I just graduated.

> ERIC
> Really, so did I.

> CHRISTINA
> Oh yeah, in what?

> ERIC
> Radio communications.

> CHRISTINA
> So, is that what you do?

> ERIC
> That's what I'd like to do. I do a little freelance deejay stuff, but right now I'm just driving a cab.

> CHRISTINA
> I thought you might do something like that.

ERIC
Drive a cab?

CHRISTINA
No, do something where you use your voice.

ERIC
Why?

CHRISTINA
Oh, I don't know why. Because you're easy to listen to.

42. **Interior. Eric's apartment. Day.**
ERIC *lies on his bed, flicking his light on and off. His voice, as if heard in his head, is heard over this scene.*

ERIC
Because of my voice, eh?

The light flicks on and off.

ERIC
I just need to find a structure.

43. **Exterior. Field. Day.**
The conversation continues.

CHRISTINA
What do you mean?

ERIC
I waste so much time. My days just slip by.

CHRISTINA
Isn't that what days are supposed to do?

44. Interior. Eric's apartment. Day.

ERIC *gets up, does his pants up and heads out the door into the hallway that leads into Exotica. His apartment is right across the hallway. The conversation still continues over.*

>ERIC
>Not if you want to make something of yourself.

>CHRISTINA
>And what do you want to make of yourself?

>ERIC
>I don't know. I just feel that I was meant to do something with my time. Otherwise I wouldn't be thinking this way. I'd be able to just continue what I was doing.

Once out in the hallway ERIC *meets* CHRISTINA *face to face. They stare intensely at each other but don't say a word.*

45. Exterior. Field. Day.

>CHRISTINA
>Do you have a lot of friends?

>ERIC
>Not really. Do you?

>CHRISTINA
>No.

46. Interior. Exotica. Day.

ERIC *and* CHRISTINA *still stare at each other. They do not speak. The conversation continues to be heard over this scene.*

>CHRISTINA
>Do you ever feel like you need a friend?

ERIC
Yeah, sometimes.

47. Exterior. Field. Day.

CHRISTINA
When?

ERIC
Like right now.

CHRISTINA
Why?

ERIC
Because I just met you ... and I feel like telling someone.

48. Interior. Exotica. Day.
ERIC *finally breaks the gaze and heads outside onto the roof.* CHRISTINA *walks off into the club and we follow* ERIC *outside.*

49. Interior. Exotica. Zoe's office. Day.
ZOE *is going through her many wigs and dresses in her cupboard.*

ZOE
No way, no way, no way.

CHRISTINA *walks in.*

ZOE
Hi.

CHRISTINA
Hi.

ZOE
Jesus.

CHRISTINA
What's the matter?

ZOE
What's the matter. Her wigs, her clothes. Sometimes I feel like just throwing them all away.

CHRISTINA
What are you looking for, Zoe? I mean is this where you see your future?

ZOE
My future? ... The club? ... When mom died, my immediate idea was to get rid of the place. Just sell it. I never thought it would have any interest for me.

CHRISTINA
So why did it?

ZOE
I used to be very shy as a child. I used to watch my mother for hours, just admiring her sense of freedom. So when the opportunity came up, I thought I would take on the challenge.

CHRISTINA
So you feel better about adopting her options rather than creating your own?

ZOE
I have created my own options too.

CHRISTINA
Oh, I know. (*takes something out of her bag*) It's your contract for the baby with Eric. I found it.

                    ZOE
Does he know?

                    CHRISTINA
I would hope so. Otherwise he might just think I'm disgusted with him for no particular reason.

                    ZOE
Look, I really desperately needed this child. It just worked out with Eric. I didn't mean to hurt you.

CHRISTINA *walks towards the other end of* ZOE's *office, which leads into the private observatory hallway where we have seen* ERIC *stand.*

                    CHRISTINA
You know, I remember when your mother built this hallway. She built it for this very rich man who used to come here. He used to get off watching us dance for other guys so he actually paid her to construct this very special place that he could watch us from. Your mother never told us that. She said it was to protect us, so she could patrol things. And I believed her. Until Eric told me the truth.

                    ZOE
Why did you believe him?

                    CHRISTINA
I made a choice. And Eric promised me he would never lie to me.

50. Interior. Opera house. Night.
THOMAS *sits with yet another attractive young man. He stares at the man's crotch and returns his gaze to the ballet.*

51. Interior. Exotica. Night.

CHRISTINA *is dancing for* FRANCIS *on the balcony.*

> FRANCIS
> How could anyone hurt you? Take you away from me? How could anyone?

FRANCIS *once again gets up from the table, upset, and heads into the bathroom. As usual,* ERIC *has been watching this exchange and he goes to follow* FRANCIS.

52. Interior. Thomas's apartment. Night.

THOMAS *and the man from the ballet, who we recognize as* IAN *from airport customs, are back at* THOMAS's *apartment.* THOMAS *makes drinks while* IAN *looks at the incubator.*

> IAN
> What's this machine?

> THOMAS
> It's an incubator.

> IAN
> What's it for?

> THOMAS
> What do you think it's for?

> IAN
> Eggs.

> THOMAS
> That's right.

> IAN
> Are they yours?

> THOMAS
> What do you mean?

EXOTICA

                    IAN
        Shouldn't you be sitting on them or
        something?

                    THOMAS
        Oh, well I guess I abandoned the
        nest.

THOMAS *brings* IAN *a drink.*

                    IAN
        What's inside of them?

                    THOMAS
        The eggs?

                    IAN
        Yes.

                    THOMAS
        Hyacinth macaws, if you want to
        know the absolute truth.

                    IAN
        Where did you get them?

                    THOMAS
        From very far away.

53. Interior. Exotica. Washroom. Night.

FRANCIS *is in a stall.* ERIC *comes into the bathroom and begins talking to* FRANCIS *in an affected accent.*

                    ERIC
        Check her out, eh? I said check her
        out.

                    FRANCIS
        Are you talking to me?

ERIC
Yes, I am talking to you.

FRANCIS
Check who out?

ERIC
The babe that's dancing for you. You've been giving her quite a run for your money.

FRANCIS
What do you mean by that?

ERIC
She's been dancing for you all night. And not just tonight, I've noticed you with her other nights, too.

FRANCIS
You come in here all the time?

ERIC
Yeah, all the time. Visuals, you know. It's good. She seems to have a bit of a thing for you, doesn't she?

FRANCIS
We get along.

ERIC
I'm sure you do, my friend. What do you two talk about?

FRANCIS
Oh, the usual, I guess.

ERIC
The usual? I don't think you are talking about what I would call usual.

FRANCIS
Why not?

ERIC
Because I can tell. You get pretty intense, my friend.

FRANCIS
Well, I guess that's just the way I am.

ERIC
Hey, why don't you give her a little touch.

FRANCIS
You're not supposed to touch.

ERIC
Yes, but she is into it, believe me.

FRANCIS
How do you know?

ERIC
Everybody knows, man. Trust me, my friend. Trust me. Just a little touch. Nothing too drastic. Then you will get the full experience, my friend. And you will love it, you will love it.

FRANCIS
What happens when I touch her?

Videotape footage of FRANCIS*'s wife and daughter is seen, as* FRANCIS*'s voice continues over.*

FRANCIS
What happens?

54. Interior. Exotica. Night.

Back out in the club. CHRISTINA *is dancing for* FRANCIS. *He reaches over and touches her stomach.* ERIC *has been waiting for this moment and runs over to throw him out of the club.*

ERIC
You're out of here, man! You're out of here.

ERIC *and* FRANCIS *scuffle as* ERIC *throws* FRANCIS *down the back stairwell towards the door. He tosses* FRANCIS *out into the stormy night, onto the middle of the road.*

55. Exterior. Exotica. Night.

DRIVER
Get off the road!

56. Interior. Thomas's apartment. Night.

The lights are off in the apartment. THOMAS *and* IAN *are silhouetted against the lights and the storm outside.* THOMAS *takes off his shirt.*

THOMAS
What's so funny?

IAN
It's like petting a gorilla. Was your father this hairy?

THOMAS
No, I got it from my mother. I mean, from my mother's side of the family. That's where you inherit hair patterns.

IAN
My uncle is bald.

THOMAS
On your mother's side?

EXOTICA

> IAN
> Yes.

> THOMAS
> Well, I guess I'm talking about usual patterns. There are always exceptions. That's just the way these things work.

57. Interior. Francis's car. Travelling. Night.
FRANCIS *looks awful, he is scuffed up and seems despondent.*

> TRACEY
> Shouldn't you go to the hospital?

> FRANCIS
> No, I'm fine.

> TRACEY
> You don't look fine.

> FRANCIS
> You worry about me, don't you?

> TRACEY
> You think this is normal?

> FRANCIS
> What?

> TRACEY
> What we do?

> FRANCIS
> What do we do?

> TRACEY
> That's just it. We don't speak about it.

> FRANCIS
> You know that feeling you get

sometimes, Tracey? That you didn't ask to be brought into the world?

TRACEY
Yes.

FRANCIS
Well then, who did?

TRACEY
What?

FRANCIS
If you think that you didn't ask to be brought into the world, then who did?

The car pulls into the parking lot outside TRACEY'*s apartment. It is raining, and no one is around tonight.*

FRANCIS
All I'm saying is that nobody asked you if you wanted to be brought into the world. You just ended up getting here. So the question is, now that you're here, who is asking you to stay?

FRANCIS *hands her money.*

TRACEY
Thanks.

FRANCIS
Thank you.

TRACEY
Look, are you sure you're going to be okay?

FRANCIS
Yes. Goodnight.

TRACEY
Goodnight.

58. Interior. Exotica. Zoe's office. Night.
ZOE *is talking to* CHRISTINA *and* ERIC. *She is trying to get the story straight about what happened with* FRANCIS *that evening.*

ZOE
He touched you?

CHRISTINA
He didn't want to.

ZOE
What do you mean?

CHRISTINA
I know him.

ERIC
We all know him. He's crazy about you.

CHRISTINA
Not like that.

ZOE
Why didn't you get one of the boys to handle this, Eric?

ERIC
Because I didn't think about it. I just saw him touch her, and ...

ZOE
Why didn't you just ask him to leave?

ERIC
Because he wouldn't have listened.

ZOE
How do you know that?

ERIC
Because he's in his own world, the asswipe.

ZOE
I don't know where you are both coming from. You are telling me that he touched you but he really didn't. And you are saying that you overreacted but you didn't have a choice.

ERIC
I didn't.

CHRISTINA
Why not?

ERIC
Why not? Because he touched you.

ZOE
Okay. All I'm concerned about is if he makes a case. I have to know what happened.

ERIC
We told you what happened, Zoe.

ZOE
And that is what happened?

CHRISTINA
Yeah.

EXOTICA

ERIC

Okay. Are we finished?

59. Interior. Thomas's apartment. Morning.

THOMAS *is in bed. The phone rings. We hear his answering machine answer, and* IAN*'s voice comes on.*

THOMAS
(answering machine)
Hi, this is Thomas. I'm not in at the present time, but I am in town. Please leave a message at the beep.

IAN
Good morning. You're probably not up yet so you haven't seen what I've done. I'm a customs officer at the airport. Actually, I saw you the other day when you were having your bags inspected. I know how you probably smuggled those eggs in. There's a special unit at work. I think they give them to the zoo or something. They asked me where I got them, I had to lie …

THOMAS *jumps out of bed and gets the phone.*

THOMAS
Where are they?

IAN
I took them.

THOMAS
Where?

IAN
I'd like to see you again …

60. Interior. Pet store. Day.

THOMAS *is on the phone. He is almost frantic as* FRANCIS *walks into the store.* FRANCIS*'s face is cut and bruised.*

> THOMAS
> No, they are in the country. They are definitely in the country. I just don't have them with me presently, but it doesn't mean I can't get them, and if you can just give me …

> FRANCIS
> Good morning.

> THOMAS
> Hi … okay, well, I'm here. Okay, so I'll talk to you later.

> FRANCIS
> You look like you're in worse shape than I am.

> THOMAS
> What happened to you?

> FRANCIS
> Oh, I fell down some stairs.

> THOMAS
> Are you okay?

> FRANCIS
> Well, do I look okay?

> THOMAS
> No, not really.

> FRANCIS
> Well, I'm better than I look. Here, I

> got you a coffee. I didn't know how you took it.

THOMAS
Oh, black's fine.

FRANCIS
Oh, I added cream.

THOMAS
Oh, well that's okay.

FRANCIS
No, here, have mine.

THOMAS
No, no.

FRANCIS
I insist.

THOMAS *takes the coffee. He opens it and smiles.*

FRANCIS
What is it?

THOMAS
Well, it's just that this has cream in it, too.

FRANCIS
It's milk.

THOMAS
Oh. Oh good.

FRANCIS
Well, I'll get to work.

FRANCIS *goes into the back and begins on his work. He soon begins daydreaming.*

61. Exterior. Field. Day.

A camera pans through the tall grass as ERIC*'s voice is heard over top.*

> ERIC
>
> *(voice-over)*
>
> What, what, is it? What is it that gives a schoolgirl her special innocence? Is it the way they smell? The sweet smell of their perfume, of their hair. The aroma of fresh flowers ...

62. Interior. Exotica. Day.

ERIC *sits in his emcee area. He is talking into the microphone but no one is there. He seems somewhat lost as he wanders around. His monologue continues.*

> ERIC
>
> ... and all that other stuff that hasn't been fucked up by late nights and a lot of bad food. Is it their gestures? The way they move, the way their body still holds on to some semblance of self-respect and dignity. When they wrap their beautiful legs around you, tight, holding on, looking at you, you looking at them. Or is it whatever comes out of their cute little mouths? All those questions, all that wondering. It's just, you know, they've got their whole lives ahead of them. And you've wasted half of yours away. Damn. What is it?

63. Exterior. Field. Day.

The people continue to walk through the field. ERIC *and* CHRISTINA *continue talking to each other.*

ERIC
There's this feeling I get sometimes, you know.

CHRISTINA
What sort of feeling?

ERIC
That I wasn't ever meant to be satisfied.

CHRISTINA
Satisfied with what?

ERIC
With a lot of things. It seems to me that every time I'm about to get ahold of something or someone, it's bound to slip away.

CHRISTINA
Maybe you want it to slip away.

ERIC
Maybe I want what to slip away?

CHRISTINA
The things you think you're about to have.

ERIC
What would you think about that?

CHRISTINA
As a general philosophy, or how it pertains to you?

ERIC
You think you could talk about how it pertains to me?

CHRISTINA
What do you mean?

ERIC
Well, I feel like I want you. Do you think that means you'll slip away?

64. Interior. Harold/Tracey's apartment. Morning.
HAROLD *reads the paper.* TRACEY *approaches him about* FRANCIS.

TRACEY
Dad? ... I'm not going to babysit for uncle Francis any more.

HAROLD
Babysit? You go there to practice.

TRACEY
That's absurd.

HAROLD
Why?

TRACEY
Dad, he pretends I'm still babysitting for him.

HAROLD
Why would you think that?

TRACEY
Because he's paying me.

HAROLD
To house-sit.

TRACEY
Twenty dollars an hour?

HAROLD
When did it go up?

TRACEY
He wants to believe that Lisa is still there. I make it easier for him to convince himself.

HAROLD
(rolling his wheelchair closer to TRACEY)
Francis always had strange ways to convince himself of many things. Things that never happened, things that might happen. People who did things for reasons that they didn't.

TRACEY
What has any of this got to do with me, Dad?

HAROLD
Nothing. Nothing at all.

TRACEY
So why do I have to keep going there?

HAROLD
You don't.

TRACEY
And you'll tell him?

HAROLD nods.

65. **Interior. Restaurant. Day.**
THOMAS and FRANCIS sit at a table. THOMAS is going over questions that FRANCIS has given him to ask.

THOMAS
I was in here the other night when that guy was thrown out. Why did that happen? Has he ever been thrown out before? Why do you think he would touch you? ...

FRANCIS
... Why do you think he would touch you?

THOMAS
Why do you think he would touch you? What do you think was going through his mind? ...

FRANCIS
Or ... What was he thinking? ... What's so funny?

THOMAS
Well, this is a joke, right?

FRANCIS
Not at all. If you do this favour for me, I'll do that favour for you.

THOMAS
But I'm not hiding anything.

FRANCIS
Thomas, you're hiding a smuggling operation that brings in over two hundred thousand dollars a year, probably a lot more. We've suspected you for a long time. I was just brought in to confirm what was already known. So how do you want me to report back?

All I'm asking for is a bit of help.

That's all. It's very important for me to know these things. Just ask her these questions. Do this for me and you have a clean slate.

THOMAS
This really hasn't been my day.

FRANCIS
So change things, make it your day.

66. Interior. Exotica. Night.

Things are rolling at Exotica. CHRISTINA *dances for a customer and* ERIC *emcees.*

ERIC
All you men sitting near that stage, I can see, I know what you're thinking. You're thinking that 'because I'm sitting next to that stage I'm getting the same feeling as all those guys shelling out all that cash for their own private dancer.' Well, you know, you guys want to watch, go to the movies. We're in the live-action business here gents. Okay, granted, granted—that beautiful creature writhing before you on stage, she maybe smiles at you, she winks her eyes at you, occasionally, and you may feel like a man. Is that all you guys are looking for? Is that all you want? Come on, come on. Invite one of our lovely ladies over to your table where the real action is.

CHRISTINA *comes over to* THOMAS's *table and introduces herself before dancing for him.*

CHRISTINA
Hi. Hi. I'm really sorry it took so long … I took so long. It's such a busy night. Hi. I'm Chrissy.

THOMAS
Hi. I'm Thomas.

CHRISTINA
It's nice to meet you Thomas. I like the name Thomas a lot.

THOMAS
Oh, thanks.

CHRISTINA
Are you from out of town?

THOMAS
Yes.

CHRISTINA
Where are you from?

THOMAS
Uhm, San Francisco.

CHRISTINA
Oh, you're kidding, I love San Francisco.

THOMAS
Oh, you've been there?

CHRISTINA
Yeah. I was there a couple of years ago with my debating team.

67. Interior. Francis's car. Night.

In his car, FRANCIS *listens to the conversation with a wireless remote receiver, from the wire he planted on* THOMAS. *The conversation continues in voice-over.*

THOMAS
Your debating team?

CHRISTINA
Yes.

THOMAS
I admire someone who can debate well, I mean who can debate instead of just argue. Anyone can argue, but it's a good skill ... ah ... discipline to be able to debate and stand back. Um ... that's something that you can apply in your life, outside of school ...

CHRISTINA
Yes ... ummhum ...

THOMAS
... when you meet someone ... or negotiating ...

CHRISTINA
Negotiating?

THOMAS
Well, if you have to ... if you have to ... it's a good skill to learn as opposed to cheerleading or something ...

68. Interior. Exotica. Night.

CHRISTINA *prepares to dance for* THOMAS *as the conversation continues.*

CHRISTINA
Well, that's what I say. Don't be

nervous about this, Thomas. We're going to have some fun, okay?

THOMAS
Sure. Sure.

CHRISTINA *begins her dance.* ERIC *watches.* CHRISTINA'*s back is to* THOMAS *when he starts asking the prepared questions.*

THOMAS
I was here the other night ...

CHRISTINA
What night was that?

THOMAS
The night that guy was thrown out. You were dancing for him ...

CHRISTINA
His name is Francis.

THOMAS
What happened?

She stops, turns around and looks seductively at THOMAS.

CHRISTINA
He was a bad boy.

THOMAS
What do you mean by that?

CHRISTINA
What do I mean?

THOMAS
I mean, have you danced for him before a lot?

CHRISTINA
Yes.

THOMAS
And has he ever been thrown out before?

CHRISTINA
No.

THOMAS
So, what do you think happened?

CHRISTINA
He touched me. And when you're dancing for the customer, they can't touch.

THOMAS
Yes, but why do you think he touched you last night? Has he ever touched you before?

CHRISTINA *stops dancing.*

CHRISTINA
Is this what you really want to talk about for five bucks a dance, Thomas?

THOMAS
Well, I just want to know what you think was going on in his mind.

CHRISTINA
Are you here for some kind of psychology conference?

THOMAS
Well … ah … yes, I am, actually.

She sits down with THOMAS, *eager to talk about this.*

> CHRISTINA
> He's a ... he's a very particular case.

> THOMAS
> Very particular in what way?

> CHRISTINA
> You want the full story?

> THOMAS
> Sure.

> CHRISTINA
> His daughter was murdered a couple of years ago.

69. Interior. Francis's car. Night.

FRANCIS *continues to listen on the wireless receiver. The conversation continues in voice-over.*

> CHRISTINA
> He was implicated.

> THOMAS
> For the murder?

> CHRISTINA
> Yeah.

> THOMAS
> Why?

> CHRISTINA
> I don't know. I don't really know the details. He was cleared and then they caught the guy who did it. But it's obviously had this incredible effect

on him. I mean, he's just so fucked up about it.

            THOMAS
Oh.

70. Interior. Exotica. Night.
The conversation continues.

            CHRISTINA
Thomas, Francis and I have a very special type of relationship. And I've never minded, but then he chose to violate it.

            THOMAS
Special in what way?

            CHRISTINA
Well, we've always had this under‑standing. I mean, I need him for certain things, and he needs me for certain things, and that's the way it's been.

            THOMAS
And how did he violate that?

            CHRISTINA
He violated that in his role, in what he's supposed to do for me …

            THOMAS
What's he supposed to do for you? He comes to this club. He pays you.

            CHRISTINA
Because I was doing things for him and he's done things for me …

71. Interior. Francis's car. Night.

> THOMAS
> What has he done for you?

> CHRISTINA
> *(crying)*
> ... I'm sorry. This is really stupid ...

72. Interior. Exotica. Night.

> CHRISTINA
> ... why I'm getting so emotional over the fact that he touched me, because I mean ... he was always paying me to do him this favour and ...

> THOMAS
> What favour?

> CHRISTINA
> I don't know, Thomas! Why do you want to know all this?

> THOMAS
> Well, I'm sorry but I just ...

> ERIC
> ... What is it about a schoolgirl that gives her that special innocence, gentlemen? Such a thing that you have absolutely no control over. You never have. And you never will. After this break, we'll be right back with sweet Chrissy ...

> CHRISTINA
> He's not supposed to do that.

               THOMAS
          Do what?

               CHRISTINA
          He's not supposed to ... he's not sup-
          posed to ... he can obviously see
          from his booth that I'm sitting here
          talking with a client. He's not sup-
          posed to call me when I'm talking
          with a client.

               THOMAS
          Do you have to go now?

               CHRISTINA
          Yeah. But I want to come back and
          I want to talk. But I want to move
          downstairs. I don't like it here.

               THOMAS
          Sure. Sure.

               CHRISTINA
          Okay, I'll see you soon.

CHRISTINA *leaves.* THOMAS *speaks into his hidden microphone.*

               THOMAS
          I'm going to move to the washroom.

73. **Interior. Exotica. Washroom. Night.**
THOMAS *goes to the washroom and enters a stall.* ERIC *comes in and begins to talk to him.*

               ERIC
          Hey, I've noticed you've been spend-
          ing a lot of time with that lady.

               THOMAS
          Are you talking to me?

> ERIC
> Yeah. You seem to both hit it off together.

> THOMAS
> I guess. I guess that can happen.

74. Interior. Francis's car. Night.

FRANCIS *can now hear the conversation between* ERIC *and* THOMAS *in the washroom. The conversation continues in voice-over.*

> ERIC
> So what do you guys talk about?

> THOMAS
> Things.

> ERIC
> What sort of things?

> THOMAS
> Well, this and that.

> ERIC
> This and that, eh?

75. Interior. Exotica. Washroom. Night.

> ERIC
> You know, it's amazing how you can hit it off with someone like that, isn't it? …

76. Interior. Francis's car. Night.

> ERIC
> You ever notice how some people just drift into your life like you've known them forever?

77. Interior. Exotica. Washroom. Night.

ERIC
I mean, there are some people that you can remember the moment you met them really clearly. And then there are other people that it seems like you've known them forever, even though you haven't. They become part of this continuous memory that you have of yourself. This ongoing ... Are you with me?

THOMAS
Ah, yeah, I think so.

ERIC
I mean, here you are and you're having this beautiful conversation with her, you're getting to know each other. And then there's other guys who come in here. There's this one guy who comes in here every other night or something, and he spends a few hours with her. But he never really gets to know her. Not the way you have, not the way you two ... She really seems to be herself with you.

THOMAS
Well, how do you know?

ERIC
What? That she's being herself?

THOMAS
Yeah.

> ERIC
> Because I used to be her lover.

78. Exterior. Exotica. Night.

FRANCIS *walks to the front door and tries to go inside. He is stopped by the doorman and a bouncer.*

> DOORMAN
> I'm sorry sir. I can't let you in.

> FRANCIS
> Why not? ... Look, can I at least just talk to the manager?

> DOORMAN
> You want to talk to the manager?

> FRANCIS
> Yeah.

79. Interior. Exotica. Zoe's office. Night.

ZOE *sits behind her desk talking to* FRANCIS. *The doorman and the bouncer stand guard.*

> ZOE
> You have to understand that we have very strict rules regarding this sort of behaviour.

> FRANCIS
> And I have always respected them.

> ZOE
> And this one time you didn't. Now the problem, Mr. Brown, is that this one time happened in a room full of other men who were watching. Now if I let you back into the club, what's to stop them from trying to do the same thing?

FRANCIS
I told you. Someone told me to do it.
I was set up.

ZOE
And you believed that someone? ...
Please, sit down.

The bouncer gets a chair for FRANCIS.

FRANCIS
Thank you.

ZOE
Why did you touch her?

FRANCIS
Well, I needed to make sure.

ZOE
Why? What if she let you? What would you have done?

FRANCIS
I'd have been disappointed.

ZOE
I'm not sure I understand you.

FRANCIS
That's not the way she was raised.

ZOE
You know her? Personally? There is another club I can recommend.

FRANCIS
I need to come here.

                    ZOE
            I understand that very well.

                  FRANCIS
            No, I don't think you understand.

                    ZOE
            Exotica is a special place. My mother
            was dedicated to creating a very par-
            ticular type of atmosphere, and I
            would like to maintain that.

                  FRANCIS
            You don't understand.

FRANCIS *gets up from the chair and walks over to one of the one-way mirrors looking out into the club.*

                    ZOE
            Mr. Brown, we're all aware of what
            you've gone through. You've suffered
            a lot. But you have to understand that
            Exotica is here for your amusement.
            We're here to entertain, not to heal.
            There are other places for that.

                  FRANCIS
            Other places?

Through the window FRANCIS *sees* ERIC *come out of the bathroom followed closely by* THOMAS. *He now knows who* THOMAS *was speaking to and knows who set him up.*

                    ZOE
            I can give you a list. Mr. Brown? Are
            you listening to me, Mr. Brown?

80. Interior. Exotica. Night.
It is late in the evening. THOMAS *sits at a table downstairs.* CHRISTINA

comes over and begins to dance for him again. THOMAS *once again initiates conversation.*

> THOMAS
> Ummm. I just met this man in the washroom.

> CHRISTINA
> What man?

> THOMAS
> I'm not sure. I was in a booth. I didn't really have a chance to see him.

> CHRISTINA
> So how did you meet him?

> THOMAS
> He just started talking to me.

> CHRISTINA
> And what did he say?

> THOMAS
> He said he used to be your lover.

CHRISTINA *stops.*

> ERIC
> Well, it's always a sad moment gentlemen, when the clock strikes that magic hour and we have to send you out into that long and dark and lonely night. But just remember, we're only ever just a dream away, wherever that is.

ZOE *comes along and whispers something to* CHRISTINA.

> CHRISTINA
> I have to go.

> THOMAS
> Oh okay. Um ... wait a minute

THOMAS *gets his wallet to pay* CHRISTINA.

> CHRISTINA
> Oh ... no ... Thomas, don't ...
> Thomas, please don't.

> THOMAS
> No, no. I insist. Please. (*she takes the money*) Thank you.

81. Interior. Francis's car. Night.
FRANCIS *and* TRACEY *are parked outside* TRACEY*'s apartment.*

> FRANCIS
> Your dad told me about you not wanting to babysit any more.

> TRACEY
> There's no baby to sit.

> FRANCIS
> Well, I just want you to know I understand.

> TRACEY
> Understand what?

> FRANCIS
> That this might all seem a little weird.

> TRACEY
> A little?

> FRANCIS
> I just want to thank you, Tracey.

TRACEY
For what?

FRANCIS
You've been very patient, and if you think the time has come for this to end, then I understand. (*he hands her some money*) Thank you.

TRACEY
Goodnight, Francis.

82. Interior. Exotica. Zoe's office. Night.
CHRISTINA *is upset, she is talking to* ZOE *about* ERIC.

CHRISTINA
He calls me from a table to dance, of course I expect you to do something ...

ZOE
Christina ...

CHRISTINA
And then he follows this guy into the bathroom and tells this guy that he was my lover.

ZOE
Well, he was.

CHRISTINA
It's going too far, Zoe.

ERIC *comes in and interrupts, surprising them.*

ERIC
Actually, baby, you have no idea how far it's gone. I told him to touch you. I said you were into it. It used to be

wonderful watching you dance for him, seeing how you could soothe him. It soothed me. You soothed me. Do you understand that?

CHRISTINA *gets up and begins to storm off.* ERIC *grabs at her to stop her. She loses it.*

          ERIC

Hey ... hey ...

         CHRISTINA

Don't ... don't ... don't! DON'T fucking touch me, you fucker ... Don't ...

          ZOE

... Stop that! Stop!

         CHRISTINA

Don't! Fuck off, Zoe.

          ZOE

Stop that. Stop ... Eric!

          ERIC

Chill out! Chill out!

          ZOE

Eric, come here. Don't. Get out of here. What's the matter?

ZOE *pulls* ERIC *off* CHRISTINA *and sends him out of the room. She moves towards* CHRISTINA *to comfort her, but* CHRISTINA *is like a live wire.*

         CHRISTINA

Fuck off, Zoe!

83. Interior. Pet store. Morning.
THOMAS *is pulling dead fish out of an aquarium when* FRANCIS *walks in.*

FRANCIS
Morning, Thomas.

THOMAS
What happened?

FRANCIS
I had to leave.

THOMAS
Did you hear everything?

FRANCIS
Yeah.

THOMAS
Did you know?

FRANCIS
Did I know what?

THOMAS
That she knew ... about your daughter?

(Pause)

FRANCIS
You know, when the police came to question me, they told me a lot of things. They told me that my wife was having an affair with my brother. Had been for years. They told me that I thought Lisa wasn't my daughter. They told me I thought she was Harold's.

THOMAS
Why would they say that?

FRANCIS
Because they thought I could harm her. That I would harm her. And then they found the man that did it and they let me go. And I went home. And then my wife was killed in a car accident a couple of months later. Harold was in the car. He lived.

FRANCIS *walks to the office area at the back of the store and takes the gun out of the desk drawer.*

FRANCIS
What do you think it would have taken for your father to kill someone? I'm asking because there is someone I want to kill now. I felt it last night as I listened to him in the washroom.

THOMAS
I don't understand …

FRANCIS
He set me up … to touch her.

THOMAS
Why would he do that?

FRANCIS
He took something very special from me. I've had too many special things taken away. That's why we have to go back tonight …

THOMAS
To kill him?

FRANCIS
What would you do, Thomas? What would you do?

THOMAS
Well ... I would talk to him ...

FRANCIS
I can't even get in there! What would you do? You go back. Tonight. And you have her dance for you. And then you touch her. And he'll throw you out just like he threw me out. But I'll be waiting outside with the gun ...

THOMAS
I'm not going to help you kill somebody!

FRANCIS
Not even to save a few years in prison?

THOMAS
No!

FRANCIS
Well, to help me then?

84. **Interior. Exotica. Night.**
ERIC *has obviously left.* ZOE *is at the emcee microphone introducing the dancers. She is not very good at it.*

ZOE
And that was Mirella, gentlemen, Mirella. You can have her at your own table for only $5. Thank you Mirella. And now, it's always a pleasure to announce to you our next

dancer. Gentlemen, please let's give
a big round of applause for Christina.

CHRISTINA *begins her routine on stage, dancing to 'Everybody Knows.' Her performance is lacklustre.* ZOE *gazes at* CHRISTINA. THOMAS *comes into the club and watches* CHRISTINA.

85. Exterior. Exotica. Night.
FRANCIS *moves along an alleyway towards the back door of Exotica.*

86. Interior. Exotica. Night.
THOMAS *finds a table while he watches* CHRISTINA.

87. Exterior. Exotica. Night.
FRANCIS *waits by the back door of Exotica.*

88. Interior. Exotica. Night.
CHRISTINA *continues her dance.*

89. Exterior. Exotica. Night.
FRANCIS *still waits with the gun by the back door. He hears a noise behind him and turns towards it. He begins walking towards the noise in the alley. Someone is walking towards him in the shadows. It is* ERIC. FRANCIS *slowly walks towards him, gun pointed.*

90. Interior. Exotica. Night.
CHRISTINA *has finished her performance and now table-dances for* THOMAS. ZOE *watches* CHRISTINA *from the private observatory hallway, much in the same way as* ERIC *used to.*

91. Exterior. Exotica. Night.
ERIC *walks towards* FRANCIS *who has a gun pointed towards him.*

ERIC
Don't be afraid. I know everything
about you.

FRANCIS
What do you know about me?

EXOTICA

                    ERIC
            I found her ...

                    FRANCIS
            You found who?

                    ERIC
            Your little girl.

92. Exterior. Field. Day.
ERIC *and* CHRISTINA *walk along. They see something.* CHRISTINA *nearly faints into* ERIC*'s arms. He protects her. The camera swings around to reveal the body of a little girl in a schoolgirl's uniform.*

93. Interior. Exotica. Night.
CHRISTINA *is dancing for* THOMAS. THOMAS *places his hand on her thigh.* ZOE *watches intently through the one-way mirror.* CHRISTINA *stares at the hand on her thigh.*

94. Exterior. Field. Day.
ERIC *covers* CHRISTINA*'s face as people come running.*

                    ERIC
                  (voice-over)
            I found her, man.

95. Exterior. Exotica. Night.
ERIC *and* FRANCIS *stare at each other. The moment is emotionally charged.*

                    ERIC
                   (whispers)
            I found her, man.

FRANCIS *reaches out for* ERIC *and embraces him.*

96. Interior. Exotica. Night.
CHRISTINA *takes* THOMAS*'s hand, turns it into a fist and throws it back at him. She looks at him and smiles seductively, then continues her dance.*

97. **Interior. Francis's house. Day.**

It is many years earlier. FRANCIS *is videotaping his wife and daughter. This is the videotape we have seen previously.*

> FRANCIS
> Yeah, play something happy, play something happy. *(there's a knock on the door)* Hello? Oh, I'll get it ...

FRANCIS *opens the door. A younger, less attractive* CHRISTINA *is standing there.*

> FRANCIS
> Hi, Christina.

> CHRISTINA
> Hi. I'm a little early.

> FRANCIS
> Yeah, that's okay. come on in.

98. **Interior/Exterior. Francis's car. Travelling. Evening.**

Still many years earlier. FRANCIS *is driving* CHRISTINA *home after babysitting.*

> FRANCIS
> It's difficult for me to tell because I never had much of a musical education myself but her teacher thinks she's really talented. Actually, we were thinking of buying her a better piano. An exotic baby grand. And when I mentioned 'baby grand' you know what she said to me? She said, 'Dad, isn't that a contradiction in terms?' I mean, she just never ceases to amaze me. I mean, she's eight years old, can you imagine, and she can already identify ... what do you call that?

The car pulls up in front of CHRISTINA*'s house.*

FRANCIS
Where's your mind?

CHRISTINA
I was just thinking.

FRANCIS
About what?

CHRISTINA
About the way you talk about Lisa. You get so excited. It's nice.

FRANCIS
Well, I'm sure your parents talk about you that way, too.

CHRISTINA
I don't think so.

FRANCIS
Oh, I do.

CHRISTINA
Why?

FRANCIS
Because you're a very responsible young woman.

CHRISTINA
Responsible to what?

FRANCIS
Well, to whatever it is you believe you have to do.

CHRISTINA
Like what?

FRANCIS
Well, Lisa loves it when you come over to babysit, for example. She says you really listen to her.

CHRISTINA
That's nice. She really listens to me, too.

FRANCIS
She thinks that you're not very happy. Listen, Christina, if there is ever anything you want to talk about, about what might be going on at home, or whatever, you know that I'm here, okay?

CHRISTINA
Okay … Okay.

FRANCIS *takes money out and hands it to* CHRISTINA.

CHRISTINA
Oh, no. It's okay. (*she takes it*) Thank you. You know, I really enjoy these drives home, Mr. Brown.

FRANCIS
Good. So do I.

CHRISTINA
Bye Mr. Brown.

FRANCIS
Bye.

FRANCIS *sits in the car watching as* CHRISTINA *walks down the long pathway towards her house and disappears inside.*

Filmography

1979 **Howard in Particular**
14 minutes, 16mm, black and white
A large company tries to streamline the retirement process by compressing the entire operation into six minutes ... without inviting guests to the party. Using an effective juxtaposition of objective and subjective camera angles, *Howard in Particular* examines the strange and obsessive nightmares of one such retiree and his submission to dismissal.
Director, Screenplay, Camera, Editor: Atom Egoyan
Music: Garth Lambert
With: Carman Guild, Anthony Saunders, Arthur Bennett
An Ego Film Arts Production.

1980 **After Grad With Dad**
25 minutes, 16mm, colour
After Grad With Dad examines the paranoid perceptions of a nervous young man who, upon accidentally arriving at his girlfriend's home half an hour earlier than expected, is forced to maintain a conversation with the girl's father.
Director, Screenplay, Camera, Editor: Atom Egoyan
Music: Garth Lambert
With: Alan Toff, Anthony Saunders, Lynda-Mary Greene
An Ego Film Arts Production.

EXOTICA

Filmography

1981 **Peep Show**
7 minutes, 16mm, black and white and colour
Peep Show demonstrates a form of pornography that intrudes upon a customer's more intimate desires. Using an unusual and innovative colour technique, the film manipulates the ordinary into the unexpected, culminating in a peep show in which the viewer becomes the subject of exploitation.
Director, Screenplay, Camera, Editor: Atom Egoyan
Colour Design: Anne McIlroy
Music and Sound Effects: Matthew Poulakakis, David Rokeby
With: John Ball, Claire Letemendia, David Littlejohn
An Ego Film Arts Production.

1982 **Open House**
25 minutes, 16mm, colour
A disturbed real-estate agent tries to sell a dilapidated house to a young couple. It soon becomes apparent that the agent is the son of the people who built the house, and that the entire ritual of selling is a bizarre method of sustaining pride in a household drained of self-respect.
Director, Screenplay, Editor: Atom Egoyan
Cinematography: Peter Mettler
Music: David Rokeby
With: Ross Fraser, Michael Marshall, Sharon Cavanaugh, Hovsep Yeghoyan, Alberta Davidson
An Ego Film Arts Production. Produced with the assistance of the Ontario Arts Council.

1984 **Next of Kin**
72 minutes, 16mm, colour
Catatonically unhappy with his family life, a young man named Peter Foster undergoes video therapy with his parents. One day, while studying tapes at the hospital, he sees the tapes of an Armenian family who feel guilty about surrendering their own son, while still an infant, to a foster home. Peter decides to present himself to this family as their lost son, to finally act out a role different from the one assigned to him in his own life. Filled with haunting images of travel and displacement, *Next of Kin* reveals a young WASP's response to working-class Armenian culture and discourses on the range of roles that life allows us to play.
Director, Screenplay, Editor: Atom Egoyan
Cinematography: Peter Mettler
Production Manager: Camelia Frieberg
Sound Recording: Clark McCarron
Sound Mixer: Daniel Pellerin
Art Director: Ross Nichol
With: Patrick Tierney, Berge Fazlian, Sirvart Fazlian, Arsinée Khanjian
An Ego Film Arts Production. Produced with the assistance of the Ontario Arts Council and the Canada Council.

1985 **Men: A Passion Playground**
7 minutes, 16mm, colour
Perched at the top of a playground apparatus, poet Gail Harris, dressed as a priestess, intones an intensive cataloguing of all types of romantic males. Stretched in a semi-circle below her, men dressed in garb ranging from business suits to track suits give homage to her while chanting 'men, men.' This poetic short is a riposte to the clichés of rock videos.
Director, Concept, Camera, Editor: Atom Egoyan
Poetry and Performance: Gail Harris
Music: Matthew Poulakakis, Perry Domzella
An Ego Film Arts Production.

EXOTICA

1985 In This Corner
60 minutes, 16mm, colour, television
A Toronto boxer, proud of his Irish heritage, is persuaded by the IRA to smuggle a terrorist back to Ireland with his fight crew. Questions of honour and loyalty are in the forefront of this moody thriller, which is punctuated by well-realized fight scenes of documentary-like intensity.
Director: Atom Egoyan
Producer: Alan Burke for the CBC
Teleplay: Paul Gross
Director of Photography: Kenneth Gregg
Editor: Myrtle Virgo
Music: Eric Robertson
With: Robert Wisden, Patrick Tierney, Brenda Bazinet

1987 The Final Twist
30 minutes, 16mm, colour, television
Special-effects artists stage an emergency in order to destroy their despicable boss. Working within a typically ironic Hitchcockian tale, Egoyan goes beyond the genre to create a realistic depiction of the workings in a small film-production house. Landau and MacDonald are particularly effective as the womanizing petty film tyrant and the artisan who constructs his 'final twist.'
Director: Atom Egoyan
Producer: John Slan for 'Alfred Hitchcock Presents'
Teleplay: Jim Beaver, from the story by William Bankier
With: Martin Landau, Robert Wisden, Ann-Marie MacDonald

1987 **Family Viewing**
86 minutes, 16mm, colour
This story of mistaken and found identities is set in a nursing home, a condominium and a telephone-sex establishment. Using a collection of video images — television, pornography, home movies and surveillance — the film observes the breakdown and restoration of of a dislocated family. Darkly humorous and unpredictable, *Family Viewing* is a complex journey into a world of brutality and sentiment.
Director, Screenplay, Editor: Atom Egoyan
Director of Photography: Robert MacDonald
Cinematography: Peter Mettler
Production Design: Linda Del Rosario
Production Co-ordinator: Camelia Frieberg
Editor: Bruce McDonald
Script Editor: Allen Bell
Music: Mychael Danna
Sound Design: Steven Munro
Sound Recording: Ross Redfern
Sound Mixer: Daniel Pellerin
With: David Hemblen, Aidan Tierney, Gabrielle Rose, Arsinée Khanjian, Selma Keklikian, Jeanne Sabourin, Rose Sarkisyan, Vasag Baghboudarian
An Ego Film Arts Production. Produced with the participation of the Ontario Film Development Corporation, the Canada Council and the Ontario Arts Council.

1988 **Looking for Nothing**
30 minutes, 16mm, colour, television
Pandemonium strikes an Armenian gathering celebrating multiculturalism when the Provincial Security Force attempts to crack a conspiracy against the visiting premier. This look at contemporary Canadian cultural mores features a set-piece in which security operators are made to dress in ethnic garb in order to infiltrate an official dinner.
Director, Teleplay: Atom Egoyan
Producer: Paul da Silva and Anne O'Brien for 'Inside Stories'/Toronto Talkies
Director of Photography: Andrew Binnington
Editor: Bruce Griffin
With: Aaron Ross Fraser, Damir Andrei, Arsinée Khanjian, Hrant Alianak

EXOTICA

1989 Speaking Parts

92 minutes, 35mm, colour

'I have worked in a hotel for five years. I have worked in film for ten. Both of these professions involve the creation of illusion. In one, the territory of illusion is a room. In the other, it is a screen. People move in and out of rooms. Actors move in and out of screens. *Speaking Parts* explores a terrain that moves between rooms and screens; a terrain of memory and desire. Somewhere in the passage from a room to a screen, a person is transformed into an image. I am fascinated by this crucial moment, and by the contradictions involved in making images of people.' — Atom Egoyan

Lance is a film extra looking for his first speaking role. When Clara, an idealistic television writer, checks into the hotel where Lance works, he seduces her into casting him in her current film. Meanwhile, Lance's co-worker Lisa prowls video stores, obsessively viewing and re-viewing the movies in which Lance appears as an extra. Haunting images and obsessive sexuality merge, as these three people become fatally entangled in a web of psycho-sexual desire.

Director, Executive Producer, Screenplay: Atom Egoyan
Executive Producer: Don Ranvaud
Line Producer: Camelia Frieberg
Assistant Director: David Webb
Director of Photography: Paul Sarossy
Art Director: Linda Del Rosario
Editor: Bruce McDonald
Script Editor: Allen Bell
Music: Mychael Danna
Sound Design: Steven Munro
Sound Recording: John Megill
Sound Mixer: Daniel Pellerin
With: Michael McManus, Arsinée Khanjian, Gabrielle Rose, Tony Nardi, David Hemblen, Patricia Collins, Gerard Parkes, Jacqueline Samuda, Peter Krantz

An Ego Film Arts Production. Produced with the participation of Telefilm Canada, the Ontario Film Development Corporation, Academy Pictures (Rome) and Film Four International (London).

1991 The Adjuster

102 minutes, 35mm, colour, Dolby Stereo

'I have made a film that concerns an insurance adjuster, some film censors, an ex-football player, an aspiring cheerleader, a podiatrist, an actress, a lamp merchant, a butterfly collector and the devoted staff of a large motel. Everyone is doing what they are doing for *a* reason, which is never *the* reason. I wanted to make a film about believable people doing believable things in an unbelievable way.' — Atom Egoyan

The Renders are in the adjustment business. Noah is an insurance adjuster who takes care of the psychological — and physical — needs of his shocked clients. Hera, his wife, is a cultural adjuster: she works at the Provincial Censor Board. When a bizarre couple pays them to vacate their home for a 'film shoot,' the Renders take up residence in the motel that houses Noah's clients and discover just how maladjusted their lives — and those of others — can be.

Director, Screenplay: Atom Egoyan
Co-Producer, Production Manager: Camelia Frieberg
Associate Producer: David Webb
Director of Photography: Paul Sarossy
Production Design: Linda Del Rosario, Richard Paris
Editor: Susan Shipton
Script Editor: Allen Bell
Music: Mychael Danna
Sound Design: Steven Munro
Starring: Elias Koteas, Arsinée Khanjian, Maury Chaykin, Gabrielle Rose, Jennifer Dale, David Hemblen, Rose Sarkisyan, Armen Kokorian
With: Jacqueline Samuda, Gerard Parkes, Patricia Collins, Don McKellar, John Gilbert, Stephen Ouimette, Raoul Trujillo, Tony Nardi, Paul Bettis, Frank Jefferson
An Ego Film Arts Production. Produced with the participation of Telefilm Canada, the Ontario Film Development Corporation and Alliance Communications.

EXOTICA

1992 Montréal vu par ... six variations sur un thème (Montreal Sextet)
'Episode 4: En passant': 20 minutes, 35mm, colour
A Customs Officer steals one of the luggage tags of a pictogram designer arriving in Montreal, then sketches him and adds the drawing to her collection of 'clients.' The designer sets off from his hotel with an audio tour of Montreal on his Walkman, almost running into the Customs Officer as he wanders through the city. Witty use of pictograms and a sensual response to the environment of a festive Montreal mark this as a gentle, philosophical interlude in *Montréal vu par* and in Egoyan's career.
Producers: Denise Robert, Doris Girard, Yves Rivard
Executive Producers: Michel Houle, Peter Sussman
Directors: Patricia Rozema, Jacques Leduc, Michel Brault, Atom Egoyan, Léa Pool, Denys Arcand
'Episode 4: En passant'
Screenplay: Atom Egoyan
Director of Photography: Eric Cayla
Editor: Susan Shipton
Music: Mychael Danna
Sound: Steven Munro
With: Maury Chaykin, Arsinée Khanjian

1992 Gross Misconduct
120 minutes, 16mm, colour, television
The violent life of hockey player Brian 'Spinner' Spencer was marked by drugs, infidelity and murder. Egoyan and scenarist Paul Gross turn this true story into a meditation on the codes of masculinity that delimited Spencer's career and life. Using titles such as 'Trouble in Paradise,' 'What's Bred in the Bone,' and 'Sudden Death Overtime' as chapter headings, they transform a potentially tawdry tale into an essay on the Canadian gothic male.
Director: Atom Egoyan
Producer: Alan Burke for the CBC
Teleplay: Paul Gross, from the book by Martin O'Malley
Director of Photography: Brian Hebb
Editor: Gordon McClellan
Music: Mychael Danna
With: Daniel Kash, Peter MacNeill, Linda Garanson, Doug Hughes, Lenore Zann

1993 **Calendar**

75 minutes, 16mm, colour

A Toronto photographer invites a different woman to have dinner with him each month. At the end of each meal, the guest makes a phone call to her lover and speaks passionately in a foreign language. The photographer's reveries reveal that his wife has left him for the man who guided their tour through Armenia, where they collected images for a calendar. Wildly humorous and sensual, *Calendar* is Egoyan's most emotionally direct film.

Director, Screenplay, Editor: Atom Egoyan
Co-Producer: Arsinée Khanjian
Director of Photography: Norayr Kasper
Music: Djivan Gasparian, Eve Egoyan, Garo Tchaliguian, Hovhanness Tarpinian
Sound Design: Steven Munro
Sound Mixer: Daniel Pellerin
With: Arsinée Khanjian, Ashot Adamian, Atom Egoyan
An Ego Film Arts Production. Produced with the participation of ZDF German Television and the Armenian National Cinematheque.

EXOTICA

1994 **Exotica**
103 minutes, 35mm, colour

'In telling the story of *Exotica*, I wanted to structure the film like a striptease, gradually revealing an emotionally loaded history. The characters in the film move through a series of rituals and routines that define their loneliness and sense of despair. At times these activities may seem perverse or absurd as people transform their pain into self-made myths and legends. It is my belief that human beings find nothing more absorbing than the exoticism of their own experience.' — Atom Egoyan

Director, Producer, Screenplay: Atom Egoyan
Producer: Camelia Frieberg
Associate Producer: David Webb
Director of Photography: Paul Sarossy
Production Design: Linda Del Rosario, Richard Paris
Costume Design: Linda Muir
Editor: Susan Shipton
Music: Mychael Danna
Sound Design: Steven Munro
Sound Mixer: Daniel Pellerin
With: Bruce Greenwood, Mia Kirshner, Don McKellar, Arsinée Khanjian, Elias Koteas, Sarah Polley, Victor Garber
An Ego Film Arts Production. Produced with the financial participation of Telefilm Canada and the Ontario Film Development Corporation.

Also available from Coach House Press:

Speaking Parts
Atom Egoyan
176 pp., 50 b&w photos
ISBN 0-88910-451-4

This book includes the complete script of Speaking Parts, *facsimiles of production notes and sketches, an introductory essay by Egoyan, an interview with the director and dozens of images from the film.*